Southern Holiday Lines
in
North Cornwall
and
West Devon

Alan Bennett

Published by
Runpast Publishing
10 Kingscote Grove, Cheltenham, Glos. GL51 6JX

To my wife Josephine

© Alan Bennett,
Runpast Publishing
October 1995

ISBN 1 870754 35 2

Printed by Amadeus Press Ltd
Huddersfield, West Yorkshire
Typesetting by Highlight Type Bureau Ltd
Bradford, West Yorkshire

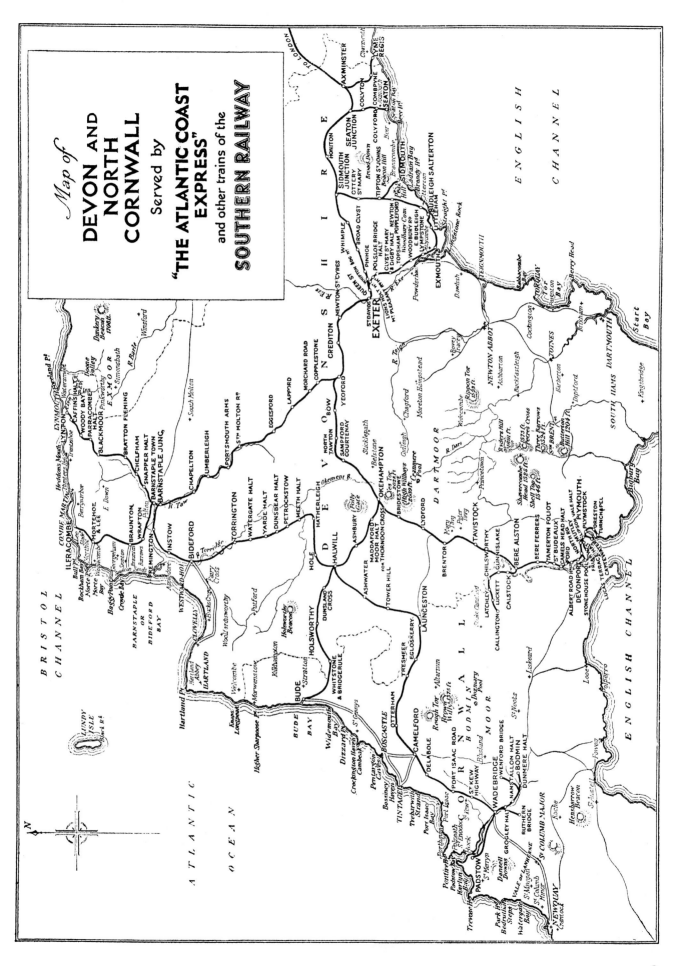

Map of
DEVON
AND
NORTH
CORNWALL
Served by
"THE ATLANTIC COAST
EXPRESS"
and other trains of the
SOUTHERN RAILWAY

A spectacular portrait of rural England and the LSWR in the landscape. An idyllic scene at Tower Hill sees T9 No. 30719 awaiting departure with the 9.56am Okehampton-Padstow on 15 July 1960. This magnificent photograph offers a poignant study of a way of life, a world that has now vanished forever. Tower Hill's remote setting also made it the site of a wartime ammunition dump, served by two sidings on the 'up', western, side of the line, this being in 1943.

R. C. Riley

Introduction

LSWR and Southern Railway interests in Cornwall and West Devon were never as extensive as their rival, the Great Western. This was not the original intention of the LSWR who looked, early on in railway development, to open a standard gauge line right through Cornwall, to the far west. In the event, Padstow became the railhead and LSWR/Southern enterprise did much for the fortunes of North Cornwall. West Devon also welcomed the presence of competition for the Great Western, the LSWR being well received in the Plymouth and Tamar Valley districts.

If the GWR boasted its prestigious 'Cornish Riviera Express', the Southern, likewise, responded with their 'Atlantic Coast Express'. Both companies, great rivals for the holiday trade, were fully aware of the potential in tourist traffic; the Great Western's story has been told in earlier volumes, this is the LSWR/Southern's experience.

Alan Bennett
August 1995

Acknowledgements

As always, many people have helped in the making of this project. In terms of research, I must give special mention to Terry Knight at the Cornish Studies Library, Redruth, and to Don Steggles of the Railway Studies Library, Newton Abbot; as ever, they have been extremely helpful and interested in the work. Both librarians offer undoubted centres of excellence. Mr R. C. Riley, not only a distinguished photographer, but an invaluable source of reference and advice, has been a friend, indeed, to me and a real source of inspiration. Thanks also to the many railway photographers who make this format of railway book possible. Here, I speak of Peter Gray for his long-term interest, Mike Esau, Neil Sprinks, Edwin Wilmshurst, Colin Hogg and, as already noted, R. C. Riley.

Stephen Mourton, as publisher, always keen to support my ideas and ensure first rate production, and Margaret Barron, for typing and deciphering beyond the call of duty, must both be thanked for their particular efforts.

Finally, my wife, Josephine, chief source of inspiration, and the driving force behind all and anything I have achieved in terms of publication.

Alan Bennett
August 1995

Contents

LONDON AND SOUTH-WESTERN RAILWAY.

OPENING OF THE NEW RAILWAY BETWEEN OKEHAMPTON AND LIDFORD.

ON MONDAY, 12TH OCTOBER, 1874, AND UNTIL FURTHER NOTICE.

UP TRAINS. — ON WEEK-DAYS.

		Only on Fridays a.m.	a.m. 1 2 3 class.	A a.m. 1 2 class	p.m. 1 2 3 class	p.m. 1 2 3 class	p.m. 1 2 3 class
South Devon Line	Launceston dep.	..	......	8 25	2 5	..	5 45
	Lifton .... „	..		8 35	2 15	.	5 55
	Coryton .... „	..		8 43	2 23	...	6 3
	Lidford ......arr.	..		8 56	2 36		6 16
	Plymouth..dep.	..	....	8 45	11 8	2 25	...
	Mutley .... „	...	....	8 50	11 13	2 30	..
	Marsh Mills „	..		9 0	11 23	2 40	..
	Bickleigh „	..		9 12	11 35	2 52	
	Horrabridge „	..		9 27	11 50	3 7	
	Tavistock .. „	..		9 40	12 3	3 20	
	Marytavy.... „	..		9 48	12 11	3 28	
	Lidford ....arr.	..		9 56	12 19	3 36	

	Only on Fridays a.m.	a.m. 1 2 3 class.	A a.m. 1 2 class	p.m. 1 2 3 class	p.m. 1 2 3 class	p.m. 1 2 3 class
Lidford ....dep.	..	7 45	10 55	2 40	4 50	7 20
Bridestowe .... „	..	7 54	11 4	2 48	4 59	7 29
Okehampton .... „	6 50	8 20	11 30	3 20	5 20	7 53
Sampford Crtny. „	6 59	8 29	11 39	3 30	5 29	8 2
North Tawton .. „	7 6	8 36	11 45	3 37	5 36	8 9
Bow ...... „	7 12	8 44	11 51	3 45	5 44	8 17
Yeoford Junction arr	7 22	8 55	12 2	3 55	5 54	8 27

		1 2 3 class.			
Change at Yeoford Jn.	Yeoford J. dep	10 40	2 11	4 39	7 13
	Barnstaple arr	12 0	3 25	5 40	8 25
	Ilfracombe	1 3	4 29	6 43	9 28
	Bideford ..	12 27	3 51	6 3	8 5
	Torrington „	12 42	4 6	6 17	9 5

	Only on Fridays a.m.	Fast Fxp. 1 2 cl	1 2 3 class	p.m.	p.m.	p.m.	p.m.
Yeoford Junction dep	7 36	9 0	9 0	12 11	4 6	6 7	8 30
Crediton........ „	7 46	9 11	9 11	12 10	4 15	6 17	8 40
Exeter........arr.	8 5	9 33	9 33	12 37	4 33	6 34	8 57
Yeovil........ „	—		11 32	12 17	2 31	6 38	8 54
Salisbury ...... „	..		12 15	1 41	3 36	7 57	
London (W'rloo) „	..		2 27	4 46	6 10	10 50	
Change at Salisbury. Southmtn arr.	..		1 51	3 36	5 30	9 37	..
Portsmth. „	..		2 19	4 10	6 15	10 30	..

A.—Third Class Tickets will be issued by the train to London, Salisbury, Yeovil, and Exeter, from Lidford and Bridestowe.

No Sunday Trains during October.

DOWN TRAINS. — ON WEEK DAYS.

		a.m. 1 2 3 class.	a.m. class.	a.m. 1 2 3 class.	a.m. 1 2 3 class.	A Fast a.m. 1 2 class.	a.m. 1 2 3 class.	Fast Expr p.m. 1 2 class.
	London (Wtrloo) dep.	..	..	...	6 45	10 45	11 45	2 10
Change at Salisbury	Portsmth dep.	..	..	...	7 55	10 50	12 30	2 15
	Southmp'n „	..	..	...	8 30	11 40	1 0	2 50
	Salisbury ......dep.	..	..	..	9 56	1 8	2 43	4 17
	Yeovil........ „	..	7 15	...	11 10	2 5	1 0	5 8
	Exeter ...... „	7 0	10 0	...	1 25	3 55		6 35
	Crediton........ „	7 25	10 26	...	2 0	4 28		7 2
	Yeoford Junction arr	7 34	10 38	...	2 10	4 38		7 12

			a.m.	a.m.	a.m.	p.m.	1 2 3 class
Change at Yeoford Junction	Torringtn dep	..	7 5	10 35	2 20	4 20	
	Bideford „	..	7 20	10 47	2 34	4 33	
	Ilfracombe „	..	6 35	10 10	2 0	..	
	Barnstaple „	..	7 47	11 12	3 0	4 56	
	Yeoford J. arr	..	9 0	12 9	4 5	6 5	

	a.m. 1 2 3 class.	a.m. 1 2 3 class.	p.m. 1 2 3 class.	p.m. 1 2 class.	p.m. 1 2 3 class.	p.m. 1 2 3 class.
Yeoford Junction dep	7 36	10 45	12 12	2 20	4 45	7 18
Bow ...... arr.	7 46	10 56	12 34	2 31	4 58	7 29
North Tawton .. „	7 52	11 4	12 56	2 39	5 4	7 37
Sampford Court. „	7 59	11 11	1 10	2 46	5 11	7 44
Okehampton.... „	8 12	11 25	1 30	3 4	5 22	7 53
Bridestowe.... „	8 30	11 43	1 56	3 20	5 40	8 11
Lidford .... arr	8 39	11 52	2 5	3 28	5 49	8 20

South Devon Line						
Lidford........dep.	9 56	12 19		3 36		9 6
Coryton .... arr.	10 8	12 31		3 48		9 18
Lifton .... „	10 16	12 39		3 56		9 26
Launceston .. „	10 28	12 51		4 8		9 38
Lidford ...... dep.	8 56		2 36		6 16	..
Mary Tavy .. arr.	9 4		2 44		6 24	..
Tavistock „	9 15		2 55		6 35	..
Horrabridge „	9 27		3 7		6 47	..
Bickleigh „	9 41		3 21		7 1	..
Marsh Mills „	9 53		3 33		7 13	..
Mutley ...... „	10 1		3 41		7 21	..
Plymouth ... „	10 7		3 49		7 29	..

A.—Third Class Tickets will be issued to Tavistock and Launceston by the train from London.

No Sunday Trains during October.

SPECIAL NOTICE.—The 6.50 a.m Train from Okehampton will run on Fridays only to Yeoford Junction, Crediton, and Exeter.

N.B.—The connections between the various Trains are not guaranteed. The classes refer only to the South Western Railway.

Waterloo Station, London.

ARCHD. SCOTT, General Manager.

Chapter One
TO PLYMOUTH

Wednesday 17 May 1876 was a memorable day for Devonport and the people of Plymouth generally. As the local press put it:

> Today will witness the completion in all its essential particulars of an undertaking which was originally projected nearly half a century since and which has taken fourteen years to finish.
>
> The long expected day has at length arrived and no one can say that Devonport did not rise equal to the occasion. Nothing could be more enthusiastic than the welcome accorded to the direction of the London and South-Western Railway Company by the town of Devonport.

Nearly three decades of service by the broad gauge South Devon company had failed to secure undivided loyalty to that camp, indeed, the arrival of standard gauge services was seen in terms of a liberation, releasing the area from an unwelcome, unsought monopoly. Devonport itself had felt slighted by the South Devon/Cornwall Railways but there were other, wider ranging factors, not least, matters of national security said to be at stake. For the latter, the two great arsenals – Devonport and Portsmouth – were separated by break of gauge, whilst in matters of commerce and trade the district had been barred from effective direct rail access to the Midlands and North. The LSWR would rectify this, ushering in a new age of prosperity through competition and service.

By way of recognition, there were the usual, inevitable celebrations – triumphal arches, an official banquet, endless speech-making, fireworks, bonfires and all the trappings of a holiday. 'Never', according to *The Western Morning News* 'was there a holiday more general than that observed in Devonport'.

The first 'up' train from Devonport left at 7.30am carrying some 200 passengers. It was witnessed by what was said to be 'many hundreds of people' and left with a salute of twenty-one fog signals. A second train was given similar treatment on its departure at 10.00am. Coming westward, the first 'down' train, the official directors train, left Exeter's Queen Street at 11.05am. This comprised a brake van, three saloons, two composites, a first class carriage and a second brake van. The locomotive was appropriately decorated for the occasion with Union Jacks, garlands of flowers and an inscription across the smokebox which read: 'Many Thanks For Your Kind Welcome'.

North Tawton was the first stop as it was necessary for the 'up' 10.00am working to cross with the official 'down' train. It was only a short stop as, indeed, was that at Okehampton where it was noted 'there were but a few people at the station'. Beyond Okehampton, the officials and guests got their first experience of Meldon Viaduct, 150 feet high carrying the line over the West Okement valley, where, soon after, the railway reached its highest point, 950 feet above sea level. Views of Dartmoor and the great tors made for a definitive feature of the journey at this stage.

At Lydford, where the LSWR standard gauge entered upon the GWR broad gauge route, via the Plym Valley, to Tavistock, it was feared that there might be an element of rivalry. It was rumoured that the GWR would charge those on the train for the remainder of the journey over their line, but, in the event, no such problems and embarrassments arose – the GWR gave instruction the previous day to allow free passage.

Tavistock provided a hearty welcome and the directors of the LSWR were given an official address upon the platform. As elsewhere the standard gauge link with other parts of Britain was stressed as being of particular value to the town. Access and mobility were foremost in thought. As the address read, albeit, with characteristic Victorian double negative:

> We would not have you to be unmindful also that the district is now largely visited by tourists to whom we hope your railway will afford convenient and ready means of access. Brought by your railway fifty-four miles nearer to the metropolis, we cannot but regard your line as the natural route to London and the North of England, and we have no doubt that whilst we do all in our power to increase the traffic on your line, you will aid the development of the district by giving us those advantages which our position and requirements necessitate.

It was an openly partisan address making clear the community's position with regard to railway access and leaving little comfort for the GWR.

Without further stop the train continued to Mutley, where, despite the thousands gathered to celebrate its arrival, only the Mayor and Corporation had access to the platform. Another short address was then offered the directors before proceeding on to Devonport itself, where the train arrived at 1.55pm. To emphasise the welcome and to demonstrate just what the standard gauge represented, a crowd of people gathered at Devonport Junction where the South Western line regained its own territory off the mixed track of the GWR. As the train passed over the junction it was noted that those gathered on the banks and the bridge together with others on the house-tops themselves cheered long and lustily to welcome the directors. The LSWR had established its identity.

At Devonport the train was met by a formidable municipal presence comprising the Mayors of Devonport, Plymouth, Okehampton, Exeter, Totnes, South Molton, Bodmin and Penzance, together with the Portreeve of Tavistock. The secretary of the Port of Plymouth Chamber of Commerce took up the issue of access and the impact of the standard gauge for the district:

> We beg to express the satisfaction we feel at realising this day our long cherished desire to bring the Port of Plymouth into connection with the rest of the narrow gauge system of England.

For the assembled guests, the LSWR represented prosperity; for the company itself, for the Port of Plymouth and for the community at large. At the celebration banquet in the specially prepared goods shed, several speakers drew comparisons between Liverpool and the Three Towns, arguing that with the good services of the LSWR and the Midland Railway working together,

Plymouth/Devonport could become the 'Liverpool of the West'.

Two consistent themes, other than that of enhanced trade, were underlined repeatedly by different speakers, these being the issue of national security and the growth of tourism. The Chairman of the LSWR, Ralph Dutton focussed upon the wider implications of the new line, bringing out the national significance:

> The opening of the new line was an event of great national importance because it connected all the great ports and arsenals of England together on one unbroken gauge.

From matters of national security he went on to tap the rising market in tourism, again making much of the fact that in conjunction with the Midland and Somerset and Dorset Railways it was possible to travel by through carriages from the Midlands and North of England:

> A large number of tourists would be attracted by the beauties of that fairest part of a fair county; everyday they saw evidence of a great desire on the part of Englishmen to become better acquainted with the beauties of their own land.

In a specific appeal to working people, the Chairman drew upon both the contrasts and the links between the Midlands and North Country industrial areas and the rural south-west. Again the emphasis was upon access and availability offered by the LSWR; upon comparison and contrast within an overall theme of unity:

> It would be of very great advantage to the mechanics of the Midlands and North of England to be enabled to leave the loom and the forge for a while and enjoy a period of relaxation in that beautiful district. The workman from the iron mills of Staffordshire might leave the rolling of

armour plates and come to Devonport and see the completed work floating upon the waters of that magnificent harbour. And the man who sat at the potter's wheel might leave there the clay to be manipulated and come down to the West of England to see the pits where the clay was dug.

This colourful appeal to working class interests was significant not only for its imagery and associations, but also for the gradual development of broader based travel, a feature of both the LSWR and the Midland Railway who were some way ahead of the GWR. Comparisons, with regard to the relative merits of the LSWR terminus at Devonport as against the less than inspired facilities at Millbay, provided by the GWR, drew the obvious comment and conclusion. The new LSWR premises were said to be 'universally admired for their elegance of design and the excellence of their construction. They are as good as they look in convenience and accommodation'.

A new road gave access to the station, the departure platform being nearest the road. The departure platform included an agent's room, first and second class refreshment room, ladies rooms, first and second class with lavatory, first and second class waiting rooms; first and second class booking offices, booking clerk's office, telegraph office, third class booking office and waiting room, parcel office and third class refreshment rooms. Construction was in dark limestone with Portland stone dressings, and polished granite. The roof was of purple slate. Iron columns supported a roof 400 feet in length, the two spans being 50 feet wide. Overall length of the platforms amounted to 500 feet, the arrival platform was laid in cement and asphalt, the departure platform being gravelled.

The goods shed to the south-east of the station was 200 feet long and 100 feet wide. Within the building itself there were two lines served by a central platform. Yard cranes and turntables were also provided. Running beneath the south-eastern corner of the goods shed was a short branch of some half a mile running down to Stonehouse Pool at the sea. Tunnelling beneath the goods shed, the branch crossed the road by the old rectory on a bridge thence following on an embankment parallel with the road at Brickfields and between this and the creek. Running under the road from Stonehouse to Devonport the line terminated in a cutting at Bluff Battery. With the intention of developing Stonehouse Pool as a dock and wharf complex the community at Devonport made its own contribution of £8,000 to the overall costs.

Staying with the theme of stations and costs, the next significant development for the LSWR and for the GWR was the opening of the joint station at North Road opened on 28 March 1877. Sir John St Aubyn, M.P. had also shown his total support for the venture in giving the land for the necessary rail access, this amounting to the value of £10,000. One of his promised rewards for such generosity was that eventually he might travel all the way to his seat at St Michael's Mount by LSWR standard gauge.

Built by Order of Parliament at 'joint' expense, 83 per cent of gross receipts for local traffic went to the GWR as owners of the line. All LSWR services were to stop at North Road, with one morning train – the first 'up' working – also stopping at Mutley. The LSWR 'down' trains also called at the latter. Passengers by LSWR were not able to book at either Mutley or North Road for any destination west of Okehampton, thereby giving the GWR the effective monopoly over that section of line. Working with status of 'running powers' the LSWR was very much at a disadvantage, there being many instances of its trains being delayed or variously obstructed by GWR activity on this shared route. At Marsh Mills where the South Devon's Tavistock branch met the main line, the line was doubled through the station, a new 'down' platform was constructed and a signal box was opened. In addition, there was extra heavy ballasting at the junction itself involving both the main and branch lines. It was also noted that considerable work had been carried out at Tavistock in connection with signalling and the permanent way.

All the main buildings at North Road were on the south side of the line – separate booking offices for LSWR and GWR trains, the refreshment rooms, waiting rooms and bookstall, for example. The buildings were of wooden construction, the platforms being in stone were paved. North Road comprised two platforms separated by two through lines occupying the original alignment of the South Devon Railway as opened in 1849. The station was modernised and extended in 1908 by the addition of two island platforms; the 'down' (GWR) side being 750 feet, the 'up' being 600 feet.

Opposite: Devonport Kings Road, the original terminus of the LSWR when it first reached Plymouth in May 1876. This view, looking eastward, shows rebuilt 'West Country' No. 34104 *Bere Alston,* leaving the station with the 2.25pm service to Waterloo. 30 September, 1961. With the opening of the independent Plymouth, Devonport and South Western Junction Railway in the early summer of 1890, Devonport became a through station. *R. C. Riley*

Above: Looking in the westward direction, another rebuilt Pacific 'Battle of Britain' Class No. 34056 *Croydon* leaves with a lightweight local working for North Road, 3 May, 1961. The spacious nature of Kings Road is evident in this view. *R. C. Riley*

TRAIN SERVICE BETWEEN NORTH ROAD AND LONDON
I. LONDON AND SOUTH WESTERN RAILWAY

LSWR services to Waterloo in these early days comprised six trains in each direction:

North Road	Waterloo	No.of Stops	Av.Speed	Remarks
a.m.	p.m.		m.p.h.	
8.33	1.47	8	44.0	Luncheon Car from Exeter; Corridor Express
10.23	3.15	4	46.9	Luncheon Car from Exeter; Corridor Express
p.m.				
12.18	5.47	11	40.9	
2.28	8.07	9	40.8	Luncheon Car from Exeter; Corridor Express
4.11	10.34	15	36.1	Luncheon Car from Exeter
a.m.				
5.09	3.35	38	22.1	

Waterloo	North Road			
a.m.	a.m.	p.m.	m.p.h.	
6.10	11.51	9	40.4	Breakfast Car to Exeter
p.m.				
8.50	3.03	15	37.1	
10.45	3.31	3	48.2	Luncheon Car to Exeter; Plymouth Corridor Express
p.m.				
1.00	6.58	11	38.5	Luncheon Car to Exeter
3.30	8.28	6	46.3	Plymouth Express
5.50	11.47	15	38.8	Dining Car to Exeter

II. GREAT WESTERN RAILWAY

The GWR provided a service of ten trains eastward and seven westward from Paddington:

North Road	Paddington	No of. Stops	Av. Speed	Remarks
a.m.	p.m.		m.p.h.	
8.33	1.30	6	45.6	Breakfast and Luncheon Car Train, via Westbury
10.43	6.00	16	33.7	via Bristol and Bath
p.m.				
*12.32	4.45	1	53.5	1st and 3rd Class Luncheon Car via Westbury
†12.38	6.50	8		Luncheon Car via Bristol and Bath
‡1.45	7.05	2		Luncheon Car via Bristol and Bath
2.10	6.45	2	49.2	Luncheon and Tea Car, via Westbury
2.20	8.30	9	40.0	Dining Car, via Bristol and Bath
3.50	10.10	8	38.8	Corridor Train, via Bristol and Bath
a.m.				
8.20	3.30	12	34.9	Sleeping Car (Sats only) via Weston-super-Mare and Bristol
a.m.				
12.15	6.45	9	37.7	Sleeping Car; except Sat. nights, via Bristol

Paddington	North Road			
a.m.	p.m.			
5.30	12.04	9	37.5	via Bath and Bristol
7.30	2.11	14	36.8	via Bath and Bristol
*10.30	2.37	0	54.5	Luncheon Car, 1st and 3rd Class; longest non-stop run in the world
11.10	3.33	1	51.5	Luncheon Car to Exeter via Westbury
11.00	3.50	2		Luncheon Car via Bath and Bristol
p.m.	a.m.			
9.50	4.34	8	36.5	1st Sleeping Car, and 3rd Class, via Bath and Bristol
midnight				
12.00	6.52	9	35.8	Sleeping Car; Monday mornings excepted, via Bath and Bristol

Cornish Riviera Express via Westbury. † Winter only. ‡ Summer only.

At North Road station heading out to the terminus at Friary, 'Battle of Britain' Class No. 34055 *Fighter Pilot,* completes its journey with a train from Waterloo, 15 July, 1956. *R. C. Riley*

On Western territory, 'West Country' No. 34033 *Chard,* brings an 'up' Waterloo service towards Mutley Tunnel and North Road from Plymouth Friary on 15 July, 1956. The train is running on the Western Region's 'up' line, on wrong line working as a result of Sunday engineering works. Climbing the bank here for Mutley Tunnel, the 'West Country' is throwing up a splendid smoke effect, but was it appreciated by local residents?! *R. C. Riley*

Comparisons and contrasts at Plymouth Laira locomotive shed on 15 July, 1956. 'West Country' Light Pacific No. 34033 *Chard* stands with Collett 'Manor' Class 4-6-0 No. 7823 *Hook Norton Manor.* Two very different styles for locomotive design. *R. C. Riley*

Laira carriage sidings with 02 No. 30225 shunting mixed stock on 27 August 1961. The construction work for the new diesel depot can be seen making good progress behind the locomotive. *R. C. Riley*

Having indicated something of the early impact and presence of the LSWR in the Plymouth area, it would be useful also to outline the stages in development whereby the company actually reached West Devon.

Exeter, as the historic gateway to the West, was the cultural and commercial capital; a focus for both the GWR and the LSWR. The latter's westward access came relatively late to the city with its train services from Salisbury beginning on 19 July 1860 as against May 1844 for the Great Western. By the end of the century, however, the LSWR network beyond Exeter was established, opening up North and West Devon and North Cornwall. Indeed, well ahead of the South Western's main line approach from Yeovil and Salisbury, the Taw Valley line to Barnstaple was opened to mixed gauge on 1 August 1854 and to Bideford by the standard gauge on 2 November 1855. The extension to Ilfracombe over formidable gradients in each direction followed on 20 July 1874.

Expansion westward began on 31 March 1864 when the Countess of Portsmouth, wife of the chairman of the Devon and Cornwall Company turned the first sod in a field on the Waterlake Estate, near Copplestone on the North Devon Railway. Under the Okehampton Railway Act of 23 June 1864, the Company was incorporated with capital of £130,000 and powers to borrow not exceeding the sum of £43,000. The company was authorised to make and maintain the Okehampton Railway being a railway commencing by a junction with the North Devon Railway in the parish of Colebrook and terminating in the parish of Okehampton.

The first section of the new line, from Coleford Junction to North Tawton, was opened from 1 November 1865. This seven mile section did not present any great difficulties, as it was reported at the time:

The county has been easy, the works light and the general conditions totally favourable.

This was from The Western Morning News; The Exeter Flying Post was less enthusiastic, downbeat even:

This piece of line in itself is very insignificant, presenting no difficulties to test the skill of the engineer, no magnificent or beautiful landscapes to attract the eye of our local artists, opens up no fresh scenes for summer picnics, and only, as yet, promising to give the archaeologists of Exeter a shorter cut than any they yet possess to Dartmoor.

Further west, the line received a much more favourable press, but it was obvious that this first section of the prospective route to Plymouth failed to inspire the Flying Post. Perhaps its loyalties or affections lay elsewhere.

Serving Bow as the only intermediate station, four miles from the junction, the line climbed westward through fertile farmland on gradients largely between 1 in 80 to 1 in 100/1 in 132. North Tawton and Bow were both on straight sections of track for the West Country and were also both on westward descents through the stations themselves, followed by steep rises. S P B Mais in his famous 'Atlantic Coast Express' holiday guide for the Southern Railway, wrote in praise of Bow as 'rich in rhododendrons giving a magnificent first view of the great tors of Dartmoor,' North Tawton, too, was 'gloriously bedecked with flowers'.

West of North Tawton, the landscape became less amenable and the company experienced problems of litigation with its rivals. The Western Morning News reported strikes, climatic delays, general panic and special distrust:

There was a very tough battle in the committee rooms of Parliament in 1865, before the opening to North Tawton. The Devon and Cornwall Company had at length shown its hand by bringing in bills for the construction of an independent line from Lydford to Milehouse, near Devonport with branches thence to Keyham, Devonport and Plymouth. The promoters were backed in this proposal by all the influence and evidence the Three Towns could bring to bear; and through failing in getting all they wanted, obtained complete running powers over the Launceston and Tavistock line to Plymouth with a right to a separate goods shed there and understandings that facilities should be given for access to Devonport also.

Although only three miles, the next section to Okehampton Road (Belstone Corner and, later, Sampford Courtenay) was not completed until 8 January 1867. A coach service provided the link with Okehampton. From Okehampton Road south-westward into Okehampton itself the landscape became more formidable. In the words of The Western Morning News reporting the opening of the line:

Immediately after passing the Okehampton road station a stiff cutting in hard slate is entered and thence the line continues through a succession of deep, bare, but not unpicturesque cuttings, and over a succession of high banks, whilst every valley opens up a wilder landscape and the gorse and fern are seen to reign, whereas but a mile or two back all was smiling in fertility.

The heavy engineering required to bring the line into Okehampton was also the subject of a report in The Western Daily Mercury:

Immediately after quitting Okehampton Road the train enters a cutting and very soon a fine glimpse of the Dartmoor Hills is obtained with Sourton Tor proudly on the right. Another cutting fifty feet deep leads to the steepest and highest embankment on the line crossing Babby Cleave, a miniature vale shut in between two sharply ascending hills. This great earthwork is 100 feet high and represents no less than 154,000 cubic yards of earth. The slope is so direct that passengers may well imagine, on the first glimpse that they are travelling over a vast wall of masonry. This neat, compact and wall-like appearance of the embankments is attributable to the rocky substance of which the gigantic masses are composed. A softer soil would have demanded a more far-spreading base. Immediately succeeding the Babby Cleave embankment comes the Corscombe Cutting and the train runs therefrom onto another great embankment 70 feet deep carrying the line across the charming Corscombe Valley. This fairy nook passed, the longest of the cuttings is entered. It is nearly three-quarters of a mile in extent and out of it 99,000 cubic yards of soil and rock had to be removed. Another heavy cutting nearly three-quarters of a mile long leads up to Exeter road bridge, (former A 30) 30 feet high from rails to roadway. Then the line makes its way onto the East Okement Valley over which it is carried by a noble granite viaduct composed of five arches of

North Tawton looking westward to Okehampton on 25 July 1964. North British diesel hydraulic No. D6342 brings in a service for Exeter. The ornate main building, the signal box, goods shed and yard are all seen here on the 'up' side. *R. C. Riley*

Another angle on North Tawton, this time, looking east as 'Battle of Britain' class, Light Pacific No. 34078 *222 Squadron,* stands at the platform with a 'down' service. The line from Coleford Junction westward to North Tawton was opened as a single track from 1 November 1865; today the route stays open for ballast traffic from Meldon, passenger trains over the reduced Exeter-Okehampton section ending in June 1972. North Tawton's footbridge enjoys a continued working life as it now does duty on the excellent Mid Hants line at Arlesford. *R. C. Riley*

40 feet span each varying in height from 47 to 50 feet. Right in front the slope of Okehampton Park covered with gorse and heather sweeps round to the town.

The report also drew attention to 'the very perceptible incline from the viaduct to the station'. Indeed, the 1 in 77 gradient was the prevailing figure south-westward from Okehampton Road.

Okehampton in its pre-railway period was considered to have been 'left out in the cold' with the opening of the South Devon Railway, since which time the town was in 'a state of chronic decline'. All this was to change from 29 August 1871. On that day a special train, hauled by two locomotives, especially decorated for the occasion, brought the directors and officials of the railway together with representatives of the LSWR to the town. Their train was met by the Mayor and Corporation of Okehampton. The streets were 'crowned by triumphal arches', the navvies were given a substantial dinner in the goods shed and there were sports and entertainments as one would expect. The official luncheon was held in a marquee near the station, and the Town Clerk read an address acknowledging that the new facilities for passengers and goods 'will be fully appreciated by the whole district and will add materially to the wealth and convenience of the neighbourhood'. Also attending was the Mayor of Devonport expressing the hope and intention for the LSWR related schemes to reach Plymouth itself. Full services began on 3 October.

Lydford, and the link with the broad gauge South Devon Railway into Plymouth, was reached on 12 October 1874. At just under ten miles this was another difficult section crossing the summit of the line, one mile west of Meldon Viaduct, and negotiating the north-western flank of Dartmoor. From Okehampton to Meldon and the summit of the line there was a climb, almost unrelenting, of 3½ miles at 1 in 77. The viaduct itself was 113 feet in height with six spans of 85½ feet to cross the West Okement Valley.

From the summit the line fell largely at 1 in 78 and 1 in 82 passing Sourton village and crossing Lake Viaduct, a granite structure of nine arches, seventy feet in height, to reach Bridestowe, a classic Dartmoor station, thence continuing at varying gradients: 1 in 200, 1 in 78 and 1 in 110 to Lydford itself. Flags were flown from Lydford Castle and a number of people turned out along the line to mark the arrival of the railway, but there was no extensive event or ceremony involved.

There were, however, serious complaints as to the poor connections between trains of the two companies. Passengers did not appreciate the wait of an hour or more for a connecting service, for example, on an eastbound journey from Plymouth to Exeter. By 1879 the Exeter-Lydford line was in the final stages of being doubled. The section from Sampford Courtenay to Meldon was inspected in January 1879. Completion was expected during the following summer.

The LSWR was anxious to extend to Plymouth as soon as possible using the mixed gauge over the South Devon Railway's Tavistock and Launceston branch. In the meantime the LSWR introduced a coach service between Tavistock and Lydford with through fares to all major destinations on the Company's network. Pressure was also applied both by the LSWR and interested parties in Tavistock to make a swift extension of the standard gauge to run trains into Tavistock whilst waiting for the larger work to Plymouth to be completed. Despite their efforts, the LSWR had to wait until May 1876 to get their all important access, as we have related earlier.

N Class No. 31855 leaves Meldon Viaduct with the 9.00am Waterloo-Plymouth working on 4 August, 1964. The quarry, supplying ballast, can be seen in the background here. A 20mph limit was imposed on the viaduct. *P. Gray*

Definite indications of change in this view as Western Region 'Warship' Class, diesel hydraulic, No. D848 *Sultan* is seen pulling away from Meldon Viaduct with the 'down' Brighton-Plymouth made up of mixed stock on 5 August 1963.   *P. Gray*

In contrast, a scene that could well date back between the Wars but is actually into British Railways' Southern Region days is offered us here as T9 4-4-0 No. 30717 climbs out of Okehampton with the 8.41am Exeter-Plymouth.   *C. Hogg*

Activity at Okehampton as 'Battle of Britain' Class No. 34080 *74 Squadron* arrives with a train from North Cornwall. An N Class 2-6-0 is seen waiting to run westward.
M. Esau

At the east end of the station 'West Country' No. 34011 *Tavistock* leaves for Exeter passing N Class No. 31853 standing on shed.
M. Esau

A T9 with an eastbound service at Plymouth Friary station in Southern Railway days. Friary, the terminus, was opened with great flourish and expectation on 1 July 1891.

Cornwall Local Studies Library

Under British Railways ownership Friary is seen here on 20 August 1958, shortly before closure. Passenger services ceased on 17 September that year. A 2-6-0 4300 Class, one of the late 1930s batch with side window cab is prominent here, these locomotives being often worked over the Southern route to Exeter. The goods shed is seen to the left of the picture and the city itself is beyond the station buildings.

E. Wilmshurst

Chapter Two
THE PLYMOUTH, DEVONPORT AND SOUTH WESTERN JUNCTION RAILWAY

Having dealt with the LSWR's initial entry to Plymouth we can now turn to the next vital stage, namely, the development of an entirely independent route to Plymouth.

When on 30 May 1890 the Plymouth, Devonport and South Western Junction Railway opened officially, the Earl of Mount Edgcumbe as Chairman made reference to the problems of operating over the South Devon line:

It is clear that the arrangement by which the traffic of a great railway company was conveyed for 23 miles on a single line of another company could never be permanent.

The severe gradient, curvature and single line sharing over a section of mixed gauge made an independent route a priority.

There had been earlier schemes for such a route as in the mid 1870's when a line was projected from Tavistock to Calstock (Gunnislake) where it would join with the East Cornwall Minerals Railway on standard gauge with a branch into Plymouth. It was, despite being ostensibly focussed on Calstock, in fact, a proposal for a second main line to Plymouth and, therefore, not at all to the liking of the GWR. Despite making headway with Parliament the scheme was eventually blocked and it failed in 1882 for want of adequate finances and support.

Two further schemes in 1883 led to success. The Devon and Cornwall Central Railway planned a route from Lydford to Calstock and the East Cornwall Minerals line on an alignment some way to the west of that eventually chosen. It was planned to cross Collocombe Down thereby saving the two local communities of Milton Abbot and Lamerton, thence via Devon Great Consol Mine, latterly the richest copper and arsenic working in Britain. Calstock and Gunnislake were to be reached over a substantial bridge, 800 yards long and 230 feet in height crossing the River Tamar. Tavistock was not included in this scheme, the line running into Devonport from Gunnislake, running to the west of Bere Alston and Tamerton Foliot. The Calstock area was considered to be of great potential for a railway. Its scope for horticulture – it was said to be superior to the Penzance district for soil and climate – and for mining and related industries were heavily stressed by its supporters. Tourism, too, was considered important.

At much the same time various local interests in Tavistock, Devonport and Plymouth began another project for the independent route. The new organisation had distinguished support in the form of the Earl of Mount Edgcumbe, the Duke of Bedford and Lord St Levan, principal landowners thereabouts. The Plymouth, Devonport and South Western Junction Railway was incorporated by Act of Parliament on 25 August 1883. Under the act the Company acquired all the interests of the Devon and Cornwall Central Railway and was empowered to build its line from Lydford to Devonport via Tavistock and Bere Alston, entering Devonport from the west along the shore of the Tamar, via St Budeaux and Ford. An intended branch for Tamerton Foliot did not materialise, but there was authorisation through the earlier schemes of the Devon

and Cornwall Central for the link to Calstock and Gunnislake finalised later under an Act of 1900 and opened on 2 March 1908.

The Duke of Bedford, Lord St Levan and the Earl of Mount Edgcumbe received £25,000 in paid shares for the land involved, they being the principal landowners. Finances were difficult at that time and although incorporated in August 1883 the first work on the line did not begin until April 1887. At the opening ceremony for the new railway on Friday 30 May 1890 the Earl of Mount Edgcumbe paid tribute to all involved. It was a significant engineering achievement and the Chairman took the opportunity to stress this and to make favourable comparisons and contrasts:

The new line goes through very heavy country involving the construction of exceedingly difficult and costly works to ensure good gradients and curves essential for the running of fast trains. The ruling gradient is 1 in 73 compared with 1 in 50 on the Launceston branch and 1 in 40 on the South Devon line. The curves also are a great improvement on those of the Launceston branch. In the new line, long cuttings have been made through solid rock, some of them 60 feet deep whilst some of the embankments are 80 feet high. There are seven viaducts of a total length of $3/4$ mile varying in height from 40 to 100 feet. The tunnels are altogether seven furlongs in length and there are 76 bridges over and under the railway.

Earlier, on 23 April, Major Mandarin inspected the line on behalf of the Board of Trade. He was obviously impressed by the workmanship and the time scale, declaring:

. . . these new lines are throughout more than ordinarily well finished and ballasted, and considering the nature of the works, the time taken in construction, three years, is remarkably short.

Minimum curvature was set at 20 chains over the new line, with one exception, namely the curve at Devonport station. The opening of the line on 30 May 1890 was something of a re-run of ceremonial and events back in May 1876 when the LSWR first reached Devonport. Officials from the Company, and those from the LSWR and Midland Railway attended. Details were given by *The Western Morning News*, a friend of the new line:

By a quarter past ten in the morning a large company including the contractors and their friends, and the representatives of the public bodies and commercial and trading interests of the Three Towns assembled under the gaily-flagged roof of Devonport station. There awaiting them was a train made up of first and second class saloon carriages. The engine was gay with flags; the exteriors of the carriages were relieved with bunches of flowers, the interiors were brightened by a profusion of rhododendron, pinks, geraniums, laburnum syringas, pansies and ferns . . . The run of 22½ miles to Lydford including two short stoppages at Bere Alston and Tavistock occupied 47 minutes, which is 12½ minutes less than the fast trains have been doing over the shorter distance of the old line.

The report noted that the passengers all enjoyed the panoramic views of the Tamar, Tavy and surrounding hills, and despite hazy light and 'a Dartmoor drizzle', a warm welcome awaited them at Lydford:

Upon arrival at Lydford the company found awaiting them the directors and officials of the owning company and of the working company, accompanied by the chairman and General Manager of the friendly Midland Company. They had travelled from Exeter in a train of saloon carriages drawn by an engine nearly covered with flags . . .

For the return journey the two trains were made into one, and, perhaps not better evidence of the ease with which the line can be worked could be afforded than the fact that a single engine drew the whole of the fifteen saloon carriages.

It was also noted that the train stopped at Brentor, where the vicar, supported by the parish constable, read an address, and again for a considerable time at Tavistock, where the staff had decorated the station with flowers, evergreens and fags. At Bere Alston the vicar, the Rev T.T. Wintle, gave an address and the Earl of Mount Edgcumbe made a speech. At St Budeaux and Ford there were large crowds whilst the Port Admiral's band and the Royal Marines were out in honour of the occasion at Devonport from where the guests were escorted to the Guildhall in Plymouth for the formal luncheon. Regular services over the line began on 2 June 1890, the LSWR trains over the shared GWR line ceasing from the previous day. Services for June 1890 comprised ten trains in each direction on weekdays, one train being to and from Tavistock/Devonport and three trains eastward on Sundays, with two workings westward.

Looking at the main engineering features of the line it is clear that every effort was made to provide for the best in performance. From Devonport, now a through station (until July 1891 services began at Mutley) the line crossed under Brickfields Bridge thence through Devonport Park Tunnel, 530 yards, thereafter, almost immediately running into Ford Tunnel, 365 yards, this actually burrowing beneath the GWR's Plymouth-Penzance main line. Ford Viaduct, 135 yards in length with seven arches of 50 feet span, was 83 feet high and built of dark blue limestone. A graceful structure astride the valley, it contrasted sharply with the GWR timber section construction to the west carrying the rival company's line.

Beyond the viaduct came Ford station described as 'a neat erection of limestone with red-brick dressings'. Good prospects for passenger traffic were predicted in 1890 as the district was developing rapidly as a residential area. Ford was designed as a passenger only station; goods were handled elsewhere.

Weston Mill Lake separated Ford and St Budeaux, the next station out of Plymouth. Described as one of the nastiest jobs of construction, the embankment across the creek took 150,000 cubic yards of shale, the mud here being 70 feet deep. Substantial filling was required. A bow string girder bridge was also incorporated into the embankment construction taking place in situ on the embankment itself. The abutments were set in place at each end when the relevant section of embankment to be bridged was removed. St Budeaux, like Ford, was also constructed of limestone with brick dressings, but the buildings were arranged on the split-site basis; the main building with offices etc being at the higher road level, the platforms being below in the shallow cutting. A covered walk-way on the 'down' eastern side connected the platform with the entrance.

From St Budeaux the line curved westward under the GWR line falling at a gradient of 1 in 75 through a deep cutting to eventually run beneath the second arch of Brunel's Royal Albert Bridge thence northward along the east bank of the Tamar. The embankment at the waterside was previously reclaimed land, but it required widening in order to accomodate the new line. By contrast, the line then passed through a deep cutting at the end of the embankment to cross Tamerton Creek. The bridge was of cast iron construction below the water line, and wrought iron above. There were seven spans of 46 feet each, the supporting columns being sunk some 55 feet to foundations. The total length of the structure was 117 yards and it was 22 feet above the high-water mark.

Warleigh Cutting separated Tamerton Creek and the River Tavy, and was also the site for the later Tamerton Foliot station opened on 22 December 1897, the station being at the southern end of the cutting. 80,000 yards of earth were removed from this cutting and the woodland nearby was the site of a navy settlement. The Tavy Viaduct was the largest engineering feature on this section, and for purposes of construction the line overall was allotted to two sets of engineers. Messrs Galbraith and Church handled the line between Plymouth and Bere Alston whilst Mr J W Szlumper took charge of the Bere Alston-Lydford section, he being the engineer appointed by arrangement with the erstwhile Devon and Cornwall Central Railway. The contractors throughout were R T Relf and Petherick, well known for their work in the West Country.

To cross the Tavy the PDSWJR provided an elegant bow-string girder bridge 483 yards in length. The central section consisted of eight bow string girders, each span measuring 130 feet. Wrought iron decking provided the basis for the track, and the iron work overall was supported by eight feet diameter cast iron colums, each one being filled with concrete and reaching 80 feet to foundation. Nine masonry spans of 80 feet completed the structure, seven being on the southern approach and two to the north. The Tavy viaduct was built on a curve of 40 chains, gave a clearance above high water of 25 feet and took two years in the making. The expenditure involved amounted to £50,000. One of the problems for construction was the isolated location, and therefore, of lack of suitable accomodation for the workforce, but the company overcame this in a somewhat novel manner. One hundred and twenty men were provided for by fitting out an old naval warship, H M S Bitterne. This was moored at the shore offering easy access to the construction site.

From the Tavy Viaduct at water level the line climbed sharply through Bere Ferrers to Bere Alston, the gradient being an unbroken 1 in 73 over the four mile section. This stretch of line also included the heaviest of the cuttings and embankments. Lockeridge embankment, for example, was 73 feet high, 220 yards in length and consumed 140,000 cubic yards of rock and filling.

With Brunel's Royal Albert Bridge as a backdrop the photographer catches M7 0-4-4T No. 30035 on the 4.05pm Plymouth-Brentor working on 31 March, 1956. This section of track was laid in on reclaimed land and offered excellent views over the Tamar.

N. Sprinks

The Plymouth portion of the *Atlantic Coast Express* runs along the level beside the River Tamar between Tamerton Foliot and St Budeaux on 31 March, 1956. This three coach portion is headed by 2-6-0 Class N No. 31834.

N. Sprinks

Bere Alston, junction for Calstock, Gunnislake and Callington seen here in August 1961. There is abundant evidence of a station at work here: the sidings and goods shed have good business and there are barrows stacked with produce on the 'up' main platform and coming off the branch train seen to the left.

R. C. Riley

Tavistock, looking towards Lydford and Dartmoor, as an up train headed by a GWR 2-6-0 4300 Class leaves the station on a bright morning in September, 1958. This was a local Plymouth-Exeter service.

M. Esau

Bere Ferrers station set between the Tavy and the Tamar had its main building and signal box on the 'down' side, likewise, its goods yard at the southern end of the station. Bere Alston later became the junction for Calstock, Gunnislake and Callington when the branch utilising the East Cornwall Minerals line opened in March 1908. Here, also, the main buildings were on the 'down' side.

Beyond Bere Alston, after further climbing at 1 in 75, the line reached a summit of sorts for the section between Tavistock and Plymouth. This was marked clearly as the point where the rivers Tavy and Walkham met, the location not surprisingly being known as Watersmeet. Given the area was one of considerable aesthetic appeal, there were calls for a station at this site and the development of pleasure grounds for excursionists.

Three principal engineering features defined the section between Bere Alston and Tavistock, these being Shilla Mill Tunnel, Shilla Mill Viaduct and Tavistock Viaduct itself. The tunnel was constructed on an S section and was 601 yards in length. It marked a falling gradient in the 'up' direction of 1 in 98. Work was completed from both ends, moving inward, the tunnel being lined with brick. Shortly after the tunnel came Shilla Mill Viaduct, an extremely graceful structure in Princetown granite of 12 spans each of 50 feet, one of the arches crossing the earlier Tavistock Canal. Mundic block was used in the initial work on the arches, and as this disintigrates rapidly, it had to be replaced as a priority. The viaduct was 230 yards in length with a maximum height of 104 feet. Climbing again, at 1 in 75, the line passed through Crowndale cutting requiring the removal of some 50,000 yards of rubble. Watts Road cutting, 50 feet deep, took 120,000 yards of soil and rock over a half-mile distance and brought the line into Tavistock itself. Prior to this an open embankment gave a panoramic view over the town and the Dartmoor heights. Tavistock Viaduct then led into the station. The viaduct was 160 yards in length and 73 feet in height; it was also built of granite.

Other than Devonport, Tavistock was the largest, most important station on the line. Set in a five acre site in the north west of the town, the facilities included booking office, parcels, waiting and refreshment rooms on the 'down' side, with a footbridge to the 'up' platform where there was also a waiting room. The signal box was also at the Lydford end of the 'up' platform, and beyond this, again on the 'up' side, was the goods shed and yard. The station buildings were of granite with blue brick facings, and the glazing drew on several colours to offer an attractive effect. Two wide approach roads served the 'up' and 'down' platforms and a new road linked the station and the town.

Heavy gradients between 1 in 80 and 1 in 75 were experienced on the climb through Brentor to Lydford. On leaving Tavistock, the line followed the course of the River Burn through the valley eventually curving northeastward to Brentor. From Wringworthy, about one mile south of the GWR station at Mary Tavy, the latter company's line from Tavistock to Launceston crosses beneath the PDSWJR and thereafter runs parallel with it, on the west 'up' side, to Lydford itself. Wallabrook Viaduct, near Wilminstone, was the main engineering feature between Tavistock and Lydford; of all the viaducts on the line, it was the smallest. At 132 yards length, the structure consisted of seven arches, each of 50 feet, the maximum height being 80 feet. Wallabrook was also a masonry structure in Dartmoor granite with arch work of concrete, this being the general practice on the line.

Brentor station served the community of North Brentor and offered access to Brent Tor itself, a landmark dominating the surrounding area. The earlier South Devon/GWR branch to Launceston chose to serve the larger neighbouring community of Mary Tavy. The main buildings at Brentor were on the 'down' side, likewise, the signal box and goods yard at the Tavistock end of the station. A final climb of a mile or so mostly at 1 in 75 brought the line to Lydford where it linked with the LSWR's route from Exeter and Okehampton. The LSWR and GWR stations were parallel here but the former had the larger presence. The main buildings and the signal box were on the 'down' side; the goods shed and yard was set between the Launceston line curved away to the west. Lydford was, of course, much extended with regard to its freight handling capacity when the wartime sidings of 1941 and the connection between the two rival companies were laid out.

Together with the obvious improvement in timings and general standards of service a special newspaper train was introduced between Plymouth and Exeter on the opening of the line. This enabled the rapid and widespread delivery of newspapers throughout the area and further endeared the LSWR locally. It remains to say, of course, that the line was worked by the LSWR from the outset 'in perpetuity at 50% of the gross receipts, with a maximum rebate of £15,650 per annum on through traffic...'

The following year, 1891, saw further progress. A 36 chain curve from Lipson Junction to Mount Gould Junction carried on an embankment enabled access to Plymouth Friary. The station here was opened to passengers on 1 July that year; the curve coming into use three months earlier. Friary emphasised the enhanced status and prestige of LSWR related interests in Plymouth. An independent terminus was hailed as a significant development for the city itself and there was great optimism for traffic and trade. The main entrance and buildings were on the 'up' or northern side of the line. There were two main line platforms and two bays and between the two main platforms was a centre line for locomotives to run round or for coaches to be stabled. The goods shed was on the 'down' or south side of the station and beyond this, again, was the tunnelled access down to Sutton Harbour.

On the approach to the Friary terminus and on the south side of the line was Plymouth Friary locomotive shed opened in 1898. There were three roads within the masonry built shed and a coaling stage and a turntable set back from the main line. Under British Rail, Southern, the shed code was 72D. In 1958, under Western control, it became 83H.

Although not directly related to the theme of 'holiday lines' there were two developments focussing upon Plymouth that should be acknowledged here. Early in 1904 the LWSR entered into competition with the GWR for the Ocean Traffic working from Stonehouse Pool Quay on the short branch from Devonport. In 1911, however, the two rival companies came to an agreement over competition in maritime business and the LSWR ceased to operate its boat traffic from Plymouth to Waterloo.

A very different form of traffic, a regular timetable of

Coach Tours over Dartmoor

FROM TAVISTOCK.

Excursionists will find amongst these the cheapest and grandest Trips in the West, as throughout the entire journey of about 26 miles magnificent panoramic views open out, and every help will be given Passengers to view the various places of note and interest at the halts and en route.

Backwell's well-appointed Char-à-Banc, or other Conveyance, will leave Tavistock, L. & S.W.R. Station, about 11.55 a.m. (in connection with the Tours announced on page 18), and will take the undermentioned routes, returning to Tavistock Station in time to enable Passengers to catch the Return Trains the same day.

No. 1 TOUR.

On Mondays and Thursdays. To Lydford, leaving Kelly College on the left, and passing en route through Mary Tavy, over Black Down and quite close to the New Army Camp at Tavy Cleave, the Dartmoor Inn and some of the finest Dartmoor Tors. At Lydford are the celebrated Waterfalls, Castle, Church (with quaint tombstone epitaphs), the famous Lydford Gorge, which, by kind permission, Excursionists by these Trips may visit on Mondays. The Char-à-Banc will stop at the Manor Hotel, Lydford, for two hours, where Luncheon and other Refreshments can be obtained. (See Note ¶). The Return Journey will be resumed via Brent Tor; on the summit of the Tor stands the ancient Church, of which a splendid view is obtained, also of the surrounding country, passing near the Great Devon Consols Mine; then on to the far-famed Morwell Rocks which tower with majestic grandeur several hundred feet above the beautiful River Tamar: here a halt of half-an-hour will be made. Leaving Morwell Rocks, a grand view of the Valley of the Tamar is seen, and the conveyance passes through much pastoral and moorland country, arriving Tavistock about 6.50 p.m.

NOTE ¶.—Passengers from Stations on the Exmouth Branch, Exeter, and intermediate Stations to Bridestowe inclusive, taking this Tour on Mondays and Thursdays, desirous of returning earlier to their destinations, may leave the Char-à-Banc at Lydford and return from that Station direct.

No. 2 TOUR

Wednesdays and Fridays. For Two Bridges and Burrator, the centre of Dartmoor, returning via Burrator. On leaving Tavistock the road rises for four miles to Cocks Tor (1,462 feet above the level of the sea), where a halt of a few minutes is made, and from this spot a grand view of the surrounding country can be obtained, including the River Tamar, Royal Albert Bridge, Saltash, Mount Edgcumbe, Staddon Heights, Plymouth Sound, Carradon Hills, in Cornwall, and Brent Tor. The conveyance passes Staple Tors, Rolls Tor, on the left, Pew Tor and Vixen Tor, on the right, over Merrivale Bridge, near the Merrivale Druidical Antiquities, also passing Great Mis Tor (1,760 feet high), King's Tor, Hessary Tor, and the model farm of the Dartmoor Prison at Princetown (where the convicts are frequently to be seen at work), arriving at the "Saracen's Head," Two Bridges, the centre of Dartmoor, about 2.30 p.m., where a halt of 1½ hours is made, and Luncheon and other Refreshments can be obtained. Near here can be seen Wistman's Wood and Crockern Tor, whereon the ancient Stannary Parliaments were held. Leaving Two Bridges at 4.0 p.m., the Return Journey is made via Princetown, Dousland, Roborough Down, Yelverton and Horrabridge, and passing Harter Tor, Black Tor, Crip Tor, Sharper Tor, Leather Tor, Narrow Tor, Sheeps Tor, to the new Plymouth reservoir, which is 80 acres in extent, there a splendid view of the Meavy and the Walkham Valley is obtained, arriving at Tavistock about 6.45 p.m.

No. 3 TOUR.

Tuesdays and Saturdays. To Dartmeet (the very heart of Dartmoor). The Char-à-Banc will run to the Model Farm of the Dartmoor Convict Prison, branching off at Rundles Stone to Princetown, one of the highest Towns in England, arriving at the Dudby Hotel, at about 1.45 p.m.; where a halt of 1¼ hours will be made for Luncheon or visits to places of interest, viz.: the Convict Prison, Hessary Tor, which is about 1,800 feet above Sea Level, and from which on a clear day a grand view of the surrounding country may be obtained, including the whole range of the Cornish Hills and Lizard Point. The Char-à-Banc will resume the journey to Dartmeet, passing the old Clapper Bridge at Okery and Two Bridges, thence along the Serpentine Valley of the Dart, with a clear view of Denner Bridge Pond, Belliver Tor, Laughter Tor, Brimpts (on the left), Prince Hall, Exworthy, Compton Tor (the remains of a Druidical Temple) (on the right), to Dartmeet, stopping there about ½ an hour; then returning to Two Bridges Hotel, where a halt will be made of ¾ an hour for Tea, etc., thence to Tavistock, arriving about 7.40 p.m.

Dartmoor: Land of Romance (LSWR, 1915)

Attractive Circular Tours
By Rail and Coach over
DARTMOOR.

EVERY WEEK-DAY
(during the Summer months)
CHEAP DAY TICKETS

are issued from the undermentioned Stations, by certain morning trains, to

OKEHAMPTON AND TAVISTOCK

To include a CIRCULAR TOUR over DARTMOOR, etc., by Char-a-Banc
or other Conveyance, as under:—

STATIONS FROM WHICH PASSENGERS ARE BOOKED.		Return Fares to Okehampton including Circular Tour.	Return Fares to Tavistock, including Circular Tour.
		Third Class. s. d.	Third Class. s. d.
Exmouth	... ...	6 0	6 9
Topsham	... ...	5 6	6 3
Exeter { Queen Street	... ...		
{ St. David's	... ...	5 0	5 9
Crediton	... ...		
Yeoford	... ...		
North Tawton	... ...	3 9	5 3
Okehampton	... ...	—	4 9
Plymouth { Friary,	... ...		
{ Mutley,	... ...		
{ North Road	... ...	5 6	4 9
Devonport	... ...		
Ford	... ...		
St. Budeaux	... ...		4 6
Bere Ferrers	... ...	} 5 0	4 3
Bere Alston	... ...		4 0
Tavistock	... ...	4 6	—
Lydford	... ...	4 0	4 0
Launceston	... ...	5 3	—
Bude	... ...	5 6	—
Holsworthy	... ...	5 0	—

Box Seats 1s. extra, to be paid the Coachman.

For full particulars, including times of departure and bookings from other
stations, see "Summer Excursions" programme, obtainable at all local stations,
or from the District Superintendent, Queen Street Station, Exeter.

'West Country' No. 34106 *Lydford* runs through the valley near Mary Tavy with a set of standard British Rail Mark One stock making up a service from Plymouth in the late 1950s. As the line climbed from Tavistock through Brentor the passengers would enjoy first-class views of Dartmoor, a feature of this route all the way to Okehampton.

M. Esau

Running the south-western fringe of Dartmoor with the Moor itself on the east side and a panoramic view of West Devon from the opposite windows, the train journey from Lydford to Okehampton was a veritable treat. This view, above Lydford, shows 'West Country' No. 34104 *Bere Alston,* before its rebuilding with the nine coaches of the daily Plymouth-Brighton service. *M. Esau*

local suburban services, based on a number of new LSWR halts increased the company's activities at Plymouth. Weston Mill Halt and Camel's Head Halt opened on 1 November 1906. Albert Road Halt, between the tunnels at Devonport opened slightly earlier, on 1 October 1906. Weston Mill closed in September 1921, Camel's Head in May 1942 and Albert Road in January 1947.

The main line services for the summer of 1914 showed sixteen departures from Friary station and twenty arrivals.

These were as follows:

PLYMOUTH FRIARY: 1914

ARRIVALS

7.26am	dep	Bere Alston	6.42am	Saturdays Only
9.04am	dep	Tavistock	8.05am	
9.35am	dep	Exeter Central	6.55am	
10.24am	dep	Tavistock	9.34am	
11.26am	dep	Exeter Central	8.40am	
12.57am	dep	Exeter Central	10.50am	
2.34pm	dep	Exeter Central	11.48am	
3.18pm	dep	Waterloo	8.50am	
3.58pm	dep	Waterloo	10.50am	July – Sept
4.06pm	dep	Waterloo	11.00am	To 30 July
5.08pm	dep	Exeter Central	2.36pm	
5.44pm	dep	Tavistock	4.53pm	
6.57pm	dep	Tavistock	6.08pm	
7.15pm	dep	Waterloo	1.00pm	
8.02pm	dep	Okehampton	6.25pm	
8.47pm	dep	Waterloo	3.30pm	Plymouth Express
9.13pm	dep	Tavistock	8.22pm	
9.56pm	dep	Exeter Central	7.20pm	
10.32pm	dep	Bere Alston	9.43pm	
12.12pm	dep	Waterloo	5.50pm	

DEPARTURES

6.15am	arr	Exeter Central	8.50am
7.42am	arr	Tavistock	8.39am
8.15am	arr	Waterloo	1.47pm
8.22am	arr	Exeter Central	11.02am
9.55am	arr	Waterloo	3.17pm
10.48am	arr	Exeter Central	1.26pm
12.05pm	arr	Waterloo	6.05pm
1.20pm	arr	Tavistock	2.25pm
2.15pm	arr	Waterloo	8.00pm
2.40pm	arr	Exeter Central	6.56pm
4.55pm	arr	Tavistock	6.00pm
5.57pm	arr	Tavistock	6.52pm
6.45pm	arr	Exeter Central	9.27pm
8.15pm	arr	Bere Alston	9.06pm
9.10pm	arr	Tavistock	10.07pm
10.55pm	arr	Tavistock	11.52pm

The inter-war years saw the introduction of more intensive services and improved facilities for tourism. Summer timetables, Saturday extras and special Sunday excursions, often linked with the National Sunday League, reflected the growth in traffic. A glance at the Summer timetable for 1932 shows that the main line west of Exeter carried an extensive service with a variety of opportunities for a wide cross-section of the people to enjoy something of a holiday break.

1932 might well be a useful point of reference as it also marked the depths of Britain's industrial problems – the Slump, economic depression and chronic unemployment. Circumstances for the Southern Railway however, were never as dire as those of its rivals. The LMS and LNER served the heavily industrial areas of Britain and depended extensively upon freight traffic as did the GWR in South Wales but it was the older, traditional heavy industries – coal, iron and steel, textiles etc that fared worst in the Depression years hitting the morale and spending power of its various communities.

By contrast, the Southern Railway overall served a relatively affluent part of Britain. The *Southern Railway Magazine* noted that population figures for its areas were increasing rapidly and that the modern industries were offering ever increasing scope for employment. Thus, the resources of those in work could be directed more to enjoyment and leisure rather than subsistence in unemployment. Also, of course, the Southern was primarily a passenger carrying railway cutting a modern and progressive image in promotional terms, not least, in its electrification schemes and the rebuilding in modern style of stations and infrastructure generally. Okehampton was a case in point locally. Here, the Southern rebuilt the signal box and modernised much of the station by the summer of 1932. To the east, of course, Exeter Queen Street was entirely rebuilt and opened as Exeter Central on 1 July 1933. It all added to the evocative imagery of the 'Sunny South Coast' and the Southern had ample opportunity to benefit from its many stylish and often varied resorts. Southern Railway excursion traffic on Sundays in the summer of 1932 saw day excursions from Waterloo, Portsmouth, Bournemouth, Christchurch, Eastleigh and Salisbury, for example, to the likes of Ilfracombe, Exeter, Plymouth, Bude, the Tamar Valley and to Dartmoor. There were also through workings onto Great Western territory as in Christchurch to Paignton, Exmouth to Bristol, Bude to Bristol and Padstow to Paignton. Locally, there were also opportunities to enjoy the West Country itself as in the Exeter and Exmouth to Plymouth, and vice versa, or the Plymouth to Bude; to Ilfracombe or Padstow, all of them reflecting the popularity and extent of the holiday trade and the initiative of the Southern in developing its obvious assets. This traffic contributed effectively to increased profits and prestige for both the Southern and the resorts.

The timetable for Summer 1932, presents the main line west of Exeter to Plymouth as being well provided with both local and long distance travel, favourably compared with services shown earlier, for 1914, and, later, for 1955.

Summer services for 1935 also saw the introduction of camping coaches: Otterham in North Cornwall, Gunnislake in the Tamar Valley and Brentor and Bridestowe for Dartmoor.

TIMETABLE SUMMER 1932
EXETER-PLYMOUTH LINE
PLYMOUTH FRIARY

ARRIVALS:

6.31am	dep	Waterloo	1.30am	
6.53am	dep	Tavistock	6.05am	
8.42am	dep	Bere Alston	7.55am	
8.54am	dep	Tavistock	7.58am	
9.21am	dep	St Budeaux	8.55am	
10.10am	dep	Exeter Queen St	7.30am	
11.18am	dep	Exmouth	7.48am	
12.30pm	dep	Bere Alston	11.49am	Not Sat.
12.43pm	dep	Bere Alston	11.59am	Sat. only
1.27pm	dep	St Budeaux	1.02pm	
2.04pm	dep	St Budeaux	1.39pm	
2.23pm	dep	Salisbury	7.58am	
2.35pm	dep	Bere Alston	1.54pm	Sat. only from 17 Sept.
2.39pm	dep	Waterloo	8.40am	Sat. only 23 July-10 Sept
3.03pm	dep	Waterloo	8.44am	Sat. only 23 July-10 Sept
3.12pm	dep	Waterloo	8.40am	Not Sats. 23 July-10 Sept
3.21pm	dep	Bere Alston	2.40pm	Sats. only
4.14pm	dep	Waterloo	11.00am	Sats. only 23 July-10 Sept
4.25pm	dep	Waterloo	11.00am	Not Sats. 18 July-9 Sept
4.33pm	dep	Waterloo	11.00am	From 12 Sept.
4.47pm	dep	St Budeaux	4.22pm	
5.15pm	dep	Tavistock	4.22pm	
5.35pm	dep	St Budeaux	5.10pm	
5.42pm	dep	Bere Alston	5.10pm	
6.12pm	dep	Exeter Queen St	3.20pm	
6.26pm	dep	Brighton	11.30am	Mon, Fri, Sats only 18 July-10 Sept.
6.52pm	dep	Waterloo	12.40pm	
7.20pm	dep	Waterloo	2.00pm	23 July-10 Sept
7.46pm	dep	Tavistock	6.50pm	
8.40pm	dep	Waterloo	3.00pm	
9.06pm	dep	Tavistock	8.15am	
10.36pm	dep	Exeter Queen St	8.07pm	Not Sats 23 July-10 Sept
10.41pm	dep	Exeter Queen St	8.15pm	Sats only 23 July-10 Sept
12.05am	dep	Waterloo	6.00pm	Not Fri/Sats.
12.09am	dep	Waterloo	6.00pm	Sats only
12.14am	dep	Waterloo	6.00pm	Fri only

PLYMOUTH FRIARY

DEPARTURES:

5.52am	arr	Salisbury	11.08am	
6.11am	arr	St Budeaux	6.39am	
7.10am	arr	Exeter	9.52am	
7.38am	arr	Tavistock	8.35am	
8.07am	arr	St Budeaux	8.33am	
8.25am	arr	Waterloo	2.09pm	
9.30am	arr	Bere Alston	10.22am	
10.05am	arr	Exeter Queen St	2.10pm	Sats only
10.10am	arr	Waterloo	4.00pm	From 12 Sept.
10.20am	arr	Waterloo	4.13pm	18 July-9 Sept. Not Sats.
10.30am	arr	Tavistock	11.29am	(Exeter 1.54pm Fri/Sats)
10.35am	arr	Waterloo	4.20pm	23 July-10 Sept Sats only
10.55am	arr	Brighton	5.22pm	Sats only 23 July-10 Sept
11.05am	arr	Portsmouth/ Waterloo	5.21pm	Not Sats. 23 July-10 Sept
12.00	arr	Waterloo	5.54pm	Fri/Sats only

12.10pm	arr	Bere Alston	12.55pm		
1.19pm	arr	Tavistock	2.20pm		
2.10pm	arr	Waterloo	8.41pm		
2.35pm	arr	Exeter Queen St	5.03pm		
3.10pm	arr	St Budeaux	3.35pm	Not Sats	
3.50pm	arr	Waterloo	10.06pm		
4.05pm	arr	Bere Alston	4.51pm		
4.31pm	arr	St Budeaux	4.58pm	Not Sats	
4.40pm	arr	Exeter Queen St	7.14pm		
5.10pm	arr	Tavistock	6.07pm		
6.17pm	arr	Tavistock	7.14pm		
7.09pm	arr	Exeter Queen St	9.48pm		
9.15pm	arr	Exeter Queen St	11.29pm	Sats only 23 July-10 Sept	
	arr	Tavistock	10.10pm	Mon-Fri	
10.50pm	arr	Tavistock	11.41pm	Sats only	

Nationalisation in 1948 did not represent any great change outwardly. Two interesting war-time developments involving connections between the Southern lines and those of the GWR were introduced at St Budeaux and at Lydford. In March 1941 a connection was laid in for both up and down main running lines on both company's rails, this being immediately south of Victoria and Ferry Road stations. At Lydford extensive wartime sidings were installed and an earlier connection between the two companies opened in 1931 and closed in November 1935 was reinstated in June 1943. This connection was immediately to the south of the station platforms.

For almost sixteen years from 1948 the Southern and Western Regions ran their independent, duplicate routes in the Plymouth district. Friary station, opened with such optimism in July 1891, closed to passengers on 15 September 1958, all Southern passenger trains then being worked to and from North Road. Some six years later, however, in September 1964 the Southern's independent route from Devonport Junction to St Budeaux was closed and all services diverted onto the Western Region line, using the wartime access to and from Victoria Road as previously opened in 1941. With the relegation of the Southern mainline from Salisbury it was inevitable that the Southern's duplicated rival route between Plymouth and Exeter would scarcely thrive under direct Western Region control as from 1963. Five years later on 5 May 1968 the Plymouth-Exeter service via Okehampton ceased as a through route. The entire section of line between Bere Alston and Meldon Quarry, west of Okehampton, was closed and lifted. It had been policy since September 1964 to make Exeter St Davids the focus for westbound Southern services with connecting DMU workings being largely responsible beyond that point. The Southern, it seems, was considered surplus to requirements. Ironically, it was the *Atlantic Coast Express*, at the beginning of that fateful decade, that excelled itself. In September 1961 the steam hauled ACE outran both the *Cornish Riviera Express* and the *Torbay Express* from Paddington. The Waterloo-Exeter timing was reduced to 2 hours 58 minutes, seven minutes faster than the *Torbay Express*. Of the original Plymouth-Exeter main line of the Southern Railway only two sections remained after May 1968; that from St Budeaux to Bere Alston serving the Gunnislake-Clastock branch and the Exeter-Okehampton service, also worked as a branch. The latter service ceased on 5 June 1972, although the line remains open for stone traffic from Meldon Quarry.

During the early Sixties Okehampton had been not only an important junction, but also the terminus for the Southern Region's 'Car Tourist Train' running at weekends, during Summer service, between Surbiton and Okehampton. Today, the cars race along the dual carriageway of the greatly improved A30 road, by-passing Okehampton without the need of car carriers; Okehampton station, on the hill below the road, is scarcely disturbed in its melancholy abandonment, except for the occasional appearance of a stone train for Meldon.

PLYMOUTH FRIARY
ARRIVALS: SUMMER SATURDAYS 1955

6.53am	dep	Tavistock North	6.00am	
7.49am	dep	Waterloo	1.15am	From 3 Sept
7.49am	dep	Waterloo	1.25am	Until 27 Aug
8.12am	dep	Tavistock North	7.20am	
8.46am	dep	Okehampton	7.00am	
10.15am	dep	Exeter Central	7.35am	
11.25am	dep	Exeter Central	8.41am	
2.13pm	dep	Tavistock North	1.22pm	
2.35pm	dep	Exeter Central	11.39am	
3.03pm	dep	Portsmouth/ Southsea	9.03am	
3.43pm	dep	Waterloo	8.54am	
4.56pm	dep	Waterloo	11.15am	
5.17pm	dep	Tavistock North	4.25pm	
6.11pm	dep	Brighton	11.30am	
6.34pm	dep	Tavistock North	5.32pm	
7.05pm	dep	Waterloo	1.00pm	
7.45pm	dep	Tavistock North	6.55pm	
8.43pm	dep	Waterloo	3.00pm	
9.12pm	dep	Tavistock North	8.20pm	
10.37pm	dep	Exeter Central	8.07pm	
12.02am	dep	Waterloo	6.00pm	(Plymouth North Road)

PLYMOUTH FRIARY
DEPARTURES: SUMMER SATURDAYS 1955

6.15am	arr	Templecombe	10.44am	(Waterloo – 1.05 pm) (Plymouth North Road)
7.00am	arr	Exeter Central	9.44am	
7.34am	arr	Tavistock North	8.31am	
8.15am	arr	Waterloo	2.15pm	
9.50am	arr	Portsmouth/ Southsea	3.37pm	
11.00am	arr	Brighton	5.22pm	
11.35am	arr	Waterloo	6.19pm	
12.08pm	arr	Tavistock North	1.09pm	
1.08pm	arr	Tavistock North	2.12pm	
2.25pm	arr	Waterloo	8.25pm	
2.35pm	arr	Exeter Central	5.08pm	
2.50pm	arr	Waterloo	10.08pm	
4.05pm	arr	Tavistock North	5.21pm	
4.40pm	arr	Waterloo	3.53am	Via Eastleigh
5.16pm	arr	Tavistock North	6.12pm	
6.14pm	arr	Tavistock North	7.16pm	
7.10pm	arr	Exeter Central	9.48pm	
9.15pm	arr	Okehampton	10.55pm	
10.30pm	arr	Tavistock North	11.24pm	

Having left Okehampton and crossed the East Okement Valley Viaduct 'Battle of Britain' No. 34066 *Spitfire* heads into a heavy cutting as it makes its way eastward with the *Atlantic Coast Express*, on 4 August, 1964. Dartmoor is behind them now as soon, passengers begin to take in the very different rolling pastoral landscapes of mid and East Devon.

P. Gray

The magnificent Calstock Viaduct seen here from the Cornish side on a glorious summer's day. A mixed train crosses the viaduct as a pleasure boat makes its way down river. Combined rail and river tickets were issued by the Southern Railway and are still, thankfully, available today as the line continues to be marketed as an outstanding tourist attraction.

C. Hogg

Chapter Three
THE BERE ALSTON – CALLINGTON BRANCH

Although the people of Callington were largely conspicuous by their absence, Monday 2 March 1908 was generally a day for celebration locally. The new Light Railway from Bere Alston on the Exeter-Plymouth main line to Callington Road, (Kelly Bray) opened to traffic, the first train leaving Kelly Bray at 7.23am and from Bere Alston at 8.33am. The main train of the day, however, arrived at the terminus at 12.45. It was extremely crowded with all those on board being in festive mood. The *Cornish Times* recorded that there were enthusiastic demonstrations at each station along the line. Welcomed by the Callington Brass Band, on the platform at Callington Road, the numerous officials and dignitaries were then taken to the Trafalgar Square Public Rooms for the official luncheon. The apparent lack of interest on the part of the community at Callington was attributed to the belief that the Portreeve was an agent for the GWR, and, as it was emphasised during the luncheon, it was the GWR that had done its best to prevent railway development in the area.

The Callington and Calstock Railway was developed from the earlier East Cornwall Minerals Railway, opened in May 1872, and built to 3 feet 6 inch gauge. This line linked the mainland district around Kit Hill, with its numerous quarries, brickworks and mining interests, with the river quays at Calstock. Total length was 7 1/2 miles, from Kelly Bray, a short distance north of Callington, to Calstock riverside, reached by means of an incline 35 chains in length at a gradient of 1 in 6. Locomotives were used on the upper section of the line from a point below the later Gunnislake station to Kelly Bray itself.

During the festivities of March 1908 the promoters of the new line looked forward to lucrative trade from the various industries along the line. They also expressed their hopes for tourism, making much of the aesthetic appeal of the line. There were also expectations of rapid development in horticulture given the recent introduction, in 1898, of the Agricultural Holdings Act doing a great deal to promote fruit and flower growing in the Tamar Valley. The rich soils and mild climate offered every opportunity for the business. Given the overall theme of this book – holiday lines – the focus on the Callington branch must be that of its tourist potential and its association with the landscape. With this in mind we can turn to a description of the line from the junction at Bere Alston to terminus high on the Cornish moors.

From Bere Alston, on the 300 foot contour, branch trains entered and left the junction from the outer face platform on the 'up', north, side of the main line. The branch trains ran westward out of the station, almost immediately entering a cutting beginning the sinuous run at 1 in 40 down to Calstock Viaduct to cross the Tamar. Initially the direction was north west but before reaching the river the line turned almost 180 degrees

Bere Alston and the branch train for Callington. 02 No. 30225 stands at the platform as the train crew and station staff take a break between duties.

M. Esau

before eventually turning north eastward to cross the viaduct. On the approach to the viaduct, maintaining the 1 in 40 gradient, the line passed through the deepest section of cutting at some 35 feet.

Calstock Viaduct, 113 feet above high water was built from broken granite and Portland cement. It comprised 12 spans of 60 feet, was 842 feet in length and reached 45 feet below the water to fix foundations. The hillside/riverside community of Calstock on the Cornish bank and the magnificent views up and down river made the viaduct a focal point for aesthetic interest on the line. Immediately off the viaduct the line entered Calstock station. The station comprised a booking office, waiting room and parcels/goods accommodation. Built of match board with corrugated iron, Calstock station also served as a crossing place – the loop was not provided with any platform facility – and was 1 mile 55 chains from Bere Alston.

From Calstock to Gunnislake the line continued its gruelling 1 in 40 ascent leaving the station on a remarkable 7 chain curve following close to the 200 foot contour at a right-angle to the station. Thereafter the line turned 180 degrees past the site of Okel Tor Mine to continue eastward above Calstock itself on an embankment, then turning north past the site of the old alignment to the incline worked by the East Cornwall Mineral Company, to the west of the line. The mixed economy of horticulture and mining is much evident on this section of the line as the railway approaches Gunnislake 4 miles 48 chains from Bere Alston.

Gunnislake station was the only other passing place on the line. It had an island platform 234 feet in length reached by a subway and was sited immediately north of the Callington-Gunnislake road, the latter community being a short distance eastward down a steep hill. To give some idea of the surrounding relief, for the route taken so far, the fall from Bere Alston to the viaduct over the Tamar was 183 feet. From the viaduct to the station at Gunnislake was some 350 feet.

From Gunnislake the line curved westward on a somewhat easier gradient of 1 in 45 to 1 in 80 to Chilsworthy, a single platform on the north side of the line and opened on 1 June 1909. The River Tamar, the Devon woodlands and the hills towards the east presented a magnificent panorama, making Chilsworthy a site of great scenic attraction. Climbing westward, Latchley, 6 1/2 miles from Bere Alston, was reached on a climb varying from 1 in 44 at Chilsworthy through sections of 1 in 53 to 1 in 200. Latchley village was some distance north of the line, the waiting room shelter being on the 'down' side. Climbing westward, the line passed Seven Stones Halt on easier gradients largely at 1 in 150 to 1 in 200. The halt was opened on 15 June 1910 in connection with the Phoenix Pleasure Grounds, the location for many day trips and outings from the area generally. Closure followed during World War One.

Luckett, the next station westward, saw the line running below the north slope of Kit Hill, where it reached 786 feet above sea level. Prior to November 1909, Luckett was known as Stoke Climsland. Between Seven Stones and Luckett, the line finally followed a short section of level running and descended at 1 in 175 through the station. The main building with a small verandah was on the 'down' side and, once again, the village was some way to the north, close to the River Tamar. Following the slope of Kit Hill, the line fell on varying gradients for much of the remaining two miles to Callington Road, nine miles fifty chains from Bere Alston.

The platform at Callington Road, renamed Callington in November 1909, was single and extended some 208 feet in length. There was a section of overall roof which also bridged the run-round loop. The platform was on the north, 'up' side of the line, likewise the locomotive shed, coaling stage and goods yard.

PLYMOUTH, DEVONPORT AND SOUTH WESTERN JUNCTION RAILWAY COMPANY.

UP TRAINS.

Callington Road, dep.	7 23	9 50	1 40	4 55	
Stokeclimsland ,,	7 32	9 57	1 47	5 2	
Latchley ,,	7 39	10 3	—	5 8	
Gunnislake ,,	7 51	10 13	2 0	5 17	6 40
Calstock ,,	8 8	10 28	2 13	5 30	6 53
Bere Alston arr.	8 15	10 35	2 20	5 37	7 0

Making the connections shewn below.

Tavistock ,,		8 39		2 39	5 45	7 49
Exeter (Queen St.) ,,		10 12	—	4 7	—	—
Waterloo ,,		1 47	—	8 7	—	—
Devonport ,,		8 47	11 8	2 57	6 20	7 31
Plymouth North Rd.,,		8 53	11 14	3 3	6 26	7 37
Plymouth Friary ,,		9 4	11 25	3 14	6 36	7 49

DOWN TRAINS.

Waterloo dep.	—	—	£ 50	11 10	1 0
Exeter Queen St. ,,	—	—	1 14	2 37	5 18
Tavistock ,,	8 8	—	2 32	4 45	6 57
Plymouth Friary ,,	7 42	11 3	1 40	4 57	6 45
Plymouth North Rd.,,	7 53	11 14	1 51	5 9	6 58
Devonport ,,	7 59	11 20	1 56	5 15	7 6
Bere Alston ,,	8 33	12 0	2 55	6 5	7 40
Calstock arr.	8 40	12 7	3 2	6 12	7 47
Gunnislake ,,	8 55	12 21	3 16	6 26	8 1
Latchley ,,	9 8	12 31	—	—	8 11
Stokeclimsland ,,	9 16	12 37	3 30	—	8 17
Callington Road ,,	9 25	12 45	3 38	—	8 25

Timetabling for 1908 showed four trains each day over the full distance of the line, with one train in each direction between Bere Alston and Gunnislake.

Gunnislake station was some distance from the town itself and separated by a steep hill. At the station there was an island platform reached by means of a subway. 02 No. 30236 waits with its mixed train for Callington, 30 August, 1954. *R. C. Riley*

An Ivatt 2-6-2T No. 41316 stands at Gunnislake with a train for Bere Alston in the latter days of steam power. The corrugated construction of the station building is also clear in this study of 28 August, 1961. *R. C. Riley*

Soundways Crossing with the 3.15pm Bere Alston-Callington mixed train on 30 August 1954. 02 No. 30236, heads up the winding gradient, the line here offering wonderful views eastward over the Tamar Valley and the landscape to Dartmoor.   *R. C. Riley*

By 1914 there were seven trains daily to Callington and six to Bere Alston. *Hints for Holidays* during the Thirties carried enthusiastic details of the train journey over the branch:

It is fortunate that such a gem of English scenery is so easily accessible to the tourist, and especially that its splendours can be enjoyed without effort from the best viewpoints imaginable – the overlooking hillsides. . . Passengers by the 'observation car' trains have these unique opportunities of viewing the wonderful panorama of the Tamar Valley hundreds of feet below and entrancing scenes of country beauty are unfolded to their gaze.

Calstock was described as 'a cameo for artists of the brush or camera, semi circled by orchard land and green sloping meadows'.

Fields and fields of narcissi or pheasant eye in the spring months and late on in the year strawberries, are next passed, lining the valley.

On the higher reaches of the line there were other equally magnificent scenes. From Luckett or Callington one was close to Kit Hill:

From the summit of Kit Hill can be enjoyed a panorama stretching from the Caradon Hills on the one side, to Brentor and Dartmoor on the other. Callington, about one mile from the station, along which many good class houses and bungalows have been built of recent years, has several hotels, and is delightfully old-fashioned.

Visitors were recommended to visit *The Land of Fruit and Honey*. This was no empty title; it had real meaning and reference. In 1936 for example, Calstock alone despatched 231,577 packages of flowers and fruit by rail, consignments described as being of record dimensions.

In the post war years the line maintained a service of eight trains to Callington or Gunnislake on weekdays in summer 1962 with a maximum of nine trains from Callington or Gunnislake. There were four trains each way over the branch on Sundays with good connections to and from Plymouth.

The 1960s, however, brought definite change. Until this time, the basic pattern or structure of services was largely unaltered giving an obvious sense of continuity. With the introduction of the 1962/63 timetable, from September 1962, Sunday service was withdrawn. Two years later steam power was withdrawn. Two years after that, in November 1966, the Gunnislake-Callington section of the branch was closed, the last train running on the evening of 5 November. With the closure, thereafter, of the main line between Bere Alston and Okehampton in May 1968, the service became that from Plymouth to Gunnislake offering eight trains in each direction. September 1970 saw the former main line section singled from St Budeaux but in recent years British Rail has made definite efforts to promote the line as one of outstanding scenic attraction and it is still possible, in season, to enjoy a combined river/rail excursion making the round trip to Calstock from Plymouth. All has not been lost, indeed. Gunnislake now has a new station on another site formerly part of the Drakewalls Mine sett and later a coal depot. The new station immediately south of the Callington-Gunnislake road has allowed for the demolition of the railway overbridge, formerly carrying the line into Gunnislake's original station of 1908.

Different generations and origins on view here as Ivatt No. 41315 stands on shed and 02 No. 30236 blows off steam with its train alongside at Callington on 30 August, 1954. Kit Hill stack, a local landmark, can be seen on the hill-top, above the 02 locomotive.

R. C. Riley

30236, a regular on the branch, is seen here, again, entering the terminus on 30 May, 1954. This higher section of the line from Gunnislake to Callington was eventually closed, in November, 1966.

R. C. Riley

The 3.57pm arrival at Callington on 30 August, 1954 offers a detailed railway view of the terminus. The overall roof is shown to good effect here emphasising the atmosphere of a small rural terminus.   *R. C. Riley*

02 No. 30225 is seen here running back on to its train prior to leaving for Bere Alston. Various features such as the signal box, an extension to the platform, and the overall roof are evident in this view.   *M. Esau*

Chapter Four
PROMOTION AND PUBLICITY

Tourism was recognised as a valuable source of income at each major stage in development by the LSWR. This was so in May 1876 when the Company first arrived; it was acknowledged again with the opening of the PDSWJR in June 1890, not least, for the access offered to Dartmoor, to the Tamar Valley and to historic Plymouth itself, and, finally, it assumed an important role in the affairs of the North Cornwall and Bude Railways, the quintessential Atlantic Coast.

Dartmoor: The Land of Romance, was a handbook published by the LSWR in the early years of this century. It offered the tourist a wide range of what were considered 'Delightful excursions by Rail, Coach and Motor Bus'. The handbook stressed the special position enjoyed by the LSWR in providing direct access to the Moor:

The principal centres for a Dartmoor holiday are the border towns – Chagford, Okehampton and Tavistock – all of which are easily reached by the London and South-Western Railway. The first named via Exeter and motor bus, and the others by corridor express trains direct. The Company's other stations to the Moor are Sampford Courtenay, Bridestowe, Brentor and Lydford. Visitors to the West Country making Exeter or Plymouth their headquarters will find all parts of Dartmoor can be visited and allow of return within the day.

Rail & Coach Trips

THROUGH OLD-WORLD PARTS.

Forty Attractive Circular Tours

Have been arranged from London (Waterloo) embracing all the principal places of interest in

DEVON & NORTH CORNWALL.

Full particulars of which are given in the Company's Tourist Programme.

ONE TICKET—ONE PAYMENT.

These Circular-Tour Tickets are most convenient, saving the trouble of re-booking; admitting the various places of interest being visited at leisure, and, with the exception of a time limit of six months, may be termed

"GO AS YOU PLEASE TICKETS."

Other tours can be arranged at the Passenger's option, upon application to the Superintendent of the Line, Waterloo Station, S.E.

DARTMOOR.

These Tourist tickets are all available for break of journey at Exeter, and those to

NORTH CORNWALL

at Okehampton also, thus allowing splendid opportunity for "doing" the sights of Dartmoor whilst touring the West Country.

Sketch Map of **L. & S. W. RY**

Travel in Comfort

By the Express Route between London (Waterloo) and the West of England.

—— UP-TO-DATE CORRIDOR CARRIAGES ——

In the principal Services, also

BREAKFAST, LUNCHEON AND DINING SALOONS,

To which passengers travelling any class have access without extra charge, except cost of meals.

SEATS RESERVED FREE.   'Phone, 3365 Hop.

TARIFF.—Breakfast, 2/6; Luncheon, 2/6; Dinners, 4-course, 3/-; 5-course, 3/6. Teas and other refreshments provided at moderate charges.

ALL TRAINS STOP AT EXETER

and for the most part call at Okehampton or Tavistock for

—— DARTMOOR. ——

EN ROUTE FOR NORTH CORNWALL

THE "LORD NELSON" WITH ATLANTIC COAST EXPRESS
LEAVING WATERLOO STATION FOR NORTH CORNWALL.

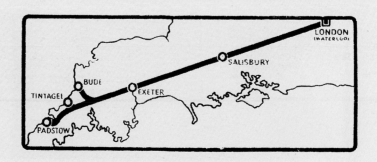

There was no doubt as to the appeal of Dartmoor; for the town dweller it offered a complete contrast to their usual surroundings – a point made wherever possible in LSWR/Southern publicity work. *The Land of Romance* made the Moor irresistible:

From its altitude and unique position about midway between two seas, Dartmoor is swept by the breezes from two Channels thus enhancing the health-giving properties of the bracing moorland air, and not the least pleasing feature so attractive to the town dweller is its wonderful solitude. One can wander from morning till night and meet only the rough-coated little ponies and flocks of sheep or perhaps one of the now famous shepherds. It must, however, be said that with the great majority the more popular method of seeing the 'sights' is from the comfortable vantage point of a coach on one of the many attractive trips over these beautiful highlands of Devon.

Tavistock and Okehampton were highlighted as the best access points to the Moor and three distinct tours were offered from each of these departure points.

Southern Railway publicity referred to Okehampton as 'Capital of the Devonshire Highlands; one of the healthiest towns in England'. At Tavistock, 'Backwell's Well Appointed Chara-Banc or other conveyance' left the LSWR station at 11.55am – the details of the tours are set out here; at Okehampton a similar well appointed Chara-Banc or other conveyance met the trains, leaving the station at 11.05am. The details are given. Cheap Day Walking Tour tickets, Special tourist and weekend tickets for first, second and third class fares were also available from Waterloo and from company stations within the county. There were also Circular Tour tickets available on weekdays during the summer months. Based on Tavistock and Okehampton, these combined rail and coach travel. The Company's bus service from Exeter to Chagford described as 'A Fascinating Route to Dartmoor' was also given prominence in the handbook.

The Okehampton-Plymouth main line offered outstanding and varied scenery much to the pride and satisfaction of the LSWR. On the higher reaches above Tavistock the line gave dramatic moorland views and stations such as Bridestowe, Lydford and Brentor enjoyed

The Land of Romance.

To omit the words "rugged and wild" from any description of Dartmoor would be nothing less than sacrilege, although the terms apply more particularly to the upper parts of the great plateau of the West. Here are mammoth upheavals of granite assuming weird and grotesque shapes, mighty tors from whose summits glorious panoramas, stretching from channel to channel, can be viewed, vast rolling downs extending away in the distance till earth and sky seem merged in one brilliant colour scheme of purple and gold and blue, and silvery streaks zig-zag across the moor in every direction as the sun glints on "many a brawling river" hasting away to add to the beauty of the garden coasts.

In this wonderful region the entranced visitor can enjoy a thousand and one emotions under the magnetic influence of the Moor in its ever-varying moods, diverting the attention in a continual round of delight.

Resting peacefully in happy valleys are old-world villages, whose folk-lore and legends have circled the Globe, such as Widecombe and its famous Fair—although, perhaps, only a west-countryman would appreciate the spirit of the quaint song, recounting the adventures of Tom Pearce's "grey mare"; and here we have the sentimental as expressed in the Spinsters', Rock, the ludicrous as Bowerman's Nose, a veritable Cruickshank study in granite, weird traditions as the "white bird" of South Zeal, and the luring by pixies of luckless "Jan Coo," the historic in Lydford recalling the good old days of Judge Jeffreys and Lydford Law, the pre-historic as told out in the strange stone circles, menhirs, dolmens and kistvaens. Startling is the effect of a solitary cross erected far from human habitation, and many the problems awakened by the collections of stones arranged in curious formation, probably of pagan origin, contrasting strangely therewith. Delightful is the experience of moving amongst the charming hill scenery, or passing through its lovely glens to the music of the turbulent hill stream tumbling down its cataracts, and for the one who is tired of the conventional holiday at some crowded resort, Dartmoor has a rare treat in store, within its area of 130,000 acres.

From its altitude and unique position, about mid-way between two seas, Dartmoor is swept by the breezes from both Channels, thus enhancing the health-giving properties of the bracing moorland air, and not the least pleasing feature so attractive to the town-dweller is its wonderful solitude. One can wander from morning till night and meet only the rough-coated little ponies and flocks of sheep, or perhaps one of the now famous shepherds. It must, however, be said that with the great majority the more popular method of seeing the "sights" is from the comfortable vantage point of a coach on one of the many attractive trips, over these beautiful highlands of Devon.

FROM OKEHAMPTON.

Well-appointed Char-à-Bancs or other conveyances meet the trains by which the Circular-Tour Tickets (announced on page 18) are issued, and leave Okehampton Station about 11.5 a.m., and the White Hart Hotel about 11.15 a.m., and run as under :—

No. 1 TOUR.

Mondays.—To Meldon Viaduct, which is over 150 feet above the Valley of the West Okement, over Sourton Down, where there is a splendid view of the Artillery Camp, Yes Tor, Black Tor, and the Island of Rocks on one side and the Cornish Hills on the other; then on to Lydford, stopping there 2 hours, giving time to view its Waterfalls, Castle, Church (with its ancient tombstone inscriptions) and Bridge of only a few feet span over a dark and apparently interminable chasm, under which the River Lyd is heard falling 60 or 70 feet beneath, also the charming Lydford Gorge (which, by kind permission, is open to the public on Mondays), then back to Okehampton, arriving there about 6.15 p.m.

No. 2 TOUR.

Tuesdays, Thursdays and Saturdays. — Through the picturesque village of Sticklepath, crossing over the River Taw at the foot of Cawsand Hill, driving close to Wheal Emily Mines along the edge of the Moor to Chagford where a wait of 1½ hours will be given; then to Rushford Mill and Castle, on the banks of the River Teign, to Sandy Park, with Whiddon Park and Cranbrook Castle on the opposite bank. Near by is the Gorge, and about half-way through is the so-called Logan Stone, supposed to be the work of the Druids. Then on to Drewsteignton (for Fingle Bridge), stopping there 1½ hours. Fingle Bridge was once an important pass of the river, fortified on one side by Prestonbury Camp, and on the other side by Cranbrook Castle; then back by way of Whiddon Down, reaching Okehampton about 8.0 p.m.

No. 3 TOUR.

Wednesdays and Fridays.—To Berrydown and Kestor Rock (one of the highest points on Dartmoor), passing close to Throwleigh and Gidleigh, stopping at Berrydown 2 hours, giving time to view the surrounding Tors, returning to Okehampton arriving there about 6.15 p.m. Nearly the whole of this route traverses the Moor.

These Tours from Okehampton open up to Excursionists views of the highest Tors and some of the choicest Hill and Dale Scenery in the Country.

Above and overleaf: Dartmoor: Land of Romance, LSWR, 1915

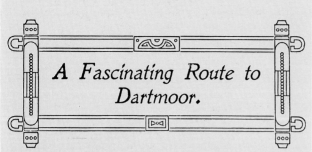

A Fascinating Route to Dartmoor.

SINCE its inauguration the service of Motor-Buses between Exeter and Chagford has proved most popular both from a point of utility and the fact that the route taken opens up some of the prettiest districts to be found in the West. The journey from the Cathedral City to the border town on the Moor occupies a little over two hours and the whole distance is full of delight to the lover of rural beauty. The 'Buses start from Exeter (Queen Street Station) and pass through many charming hamlets and peaceful old-world villages, calling amongst other places at Tedburn St. Mary, Cheriton Cross, and Crockernwell. At the latter place passengers alight for Fingle Bridge, the "Lion" of Dartmoor's beauty spots in the lovely Teign Gorge, also for Drewsteignton village near which is the Spinsters' Rock, reminiscent of Stonehenge and said to be the finest dolmen in Devon. The three upright stones are 7 feet in height, and the cross-piece 15 feet in length and 10 feet in width. Tradition credits three spinsters with having erected these remarkable stones before breakfast, why at such an hour or for what reason is left to conjecture. Bradmere Pool is also an attraction in the vicinity.

A favourite and convenient excursion to these parts is by the morning 'Bus from Exeter, returning by the evening service, which affords ample time for exploring the delights of this charming region.

Other stopping places are Whiddon Down and Sandy Park, and after about fifteen minutes' run from the last-named, the 'Bus enters the pleasant little town of Chagford on the eastern edge of Dartmoor, stopping at the Moor Park Hotel, and five minutes later reaching its terminus the Globe Hotel.

The surrounding hill scenery is very fine, and the upper reaches of the river Teign in the neighbourhood abound in scenes of unparalleled beauty, said to be the loveliest when autumn tints impart the exquisite colour schemes that only the genius of a "Widgery" can reproduce. Excellent accommodation can be obtained in the town, the first place in the West to be lighted by electricity, the necessary power being obtained from the river. Within walking distance are many noted beauty spots such as Fingle Bridge, Holy Street, Gidleigh Park, Lustleigh Cleave, Chudleigh Glen, Manaton for Becky Falls, imposing tors as Hound Tor, Hey Tor, Bel Tor, Rippon Tor and Logan Stone, the curious Bowerman's Nose and the world-renowned village of Widecombe, famous for its Fair and as the objective of the "old grey mare" and the immortal worthies who accompanied her, also as being favored with a visit in person by the devil with terrible results to Church and worshippers. Numerous stone "circles" will be found in the district, the most important being Fernworthy, Three Boys and Grey Wethers (resembling a flock of sheep). Cranmere Pool is only a few miles distant. Should the visitor be partial to the royal and ancient game there is an excellent golf course on which to indulge.

Motor-Bus Service

—— BETWEEN ——
EXETER (QUEEN STREET STATION) & CHAGFORD.

The L. & S.W. Company's Motor-Bus leaves Exeter (Queen Street Station) for Chagford every week-day morning, also immediately after arrival of CORRIDOR EXPRESS FROM LONDON leaving Waterloo Station about 11.0 a.m.

Connections are also formed with trains from Portsmouth, Southampton, Yeovil, Exmouth, Plymouth and North Devon.

As the times vary according to the season of the year, passengers should refer to the current time tables for full particulars.

The table given below shows approximately the time taken en route from Exeter to Chagford, and also applies in the reverse direction.

	Approximate time en route	Fares from Exeter.			
		Single.		Return.	
	Hrs. Mins.	s.	d.	s.	d.
EXETER (Queen Street Station) by Motor-Bus ... ... dep.	0	—		—	
Exeter (L. & S. W. R. Office, Bonhay) ... ... ,,	5	—		—	
Travellers' Rest ... ... ,,	30	0	6	—	
Tedburn St. Mary ... ... ,,	50	0	10	1	6
Cheriton Cross (for Cheriton Bishop) ... ... ,,	1 10	1	3	2	0
Crockernwell (for Drewsteignton and Fingle Bridge) ... ... ,,	1 25	1	6	2	6
Whiddon Down ... ... ,,	1 50	2	0	3	6
Sandy Park ... ... ,,	2 5	2	6	4	6
CHAGFORD { Moor Park Hotel arr.	2 20	2	6	4 * 6
{ Globe Hotel ... ,,	2 25	2	6	4 * 6

These return fares are also available in the reverse direction.

*Market Tickets at a fare of 3s. 6d. are issued from Chagford and Sandy Park to Exeter on Fridays, available for return on the day of issue only.

THROUGH TICKETS.—Through Rail and 'Bus Tickets will be issued to Chagford from principal Stations, and also from Chagford to London only, and Passengers holding such Tickets will be given seating preference over local Passengers.

LOCAL TICKETS will be issued by the Conductor. Back halves of Return Tickets are available on the day of issue and following day or from Saturday to Monday only.

STOPPING PLACES.—Should there be room on the 'Bus it will stop, if required, at any point on the journey other than the booked places for Passengers, who will pay the fare as from the previous booked stopping place. Single Tickets only are issued between intermediate stopping places, details of which are shown on bills.

CHAGFORD.—The Motor-Bus Enquiry Office at Chagford is at Mr. Webber's, The Square, where parcels may be left, seats booked, and tickets and all information obtained upon application.

---

the advantages of main line status and their close, even immediate, proximity to the Moor. These fortunate circumstances were not lost on Southern Railway publicists who made the most of the situation. S P B Mais considered the Okehampton-Plymouth journey as 'probably the finest panorama of England obtainable from any railway carriage window'. Positive comparisons with the West Highland line were also offered.

Bridestowe was the nearest station for some of Dartmoor's most awesome, spectacular landscapes, especially the high moorland. *Hints for Holidays* gave the details:

Bridestowe is immediately beyond Okehampton and close to the station are Sourton Tors, High Willhays (1039 feet) and Yes Tor (2028 feet) the highest parts of Dartmoor, also the greatest altitude in England, south of the Cumberland fells. Magnificent prospects are commanded from coast to coast. Amicombe Hill is 1920 feet high and there are the stones known

as Bishop Bronescombe's Loaf and Cheese, which legend avers to have been originally bread and cheese proffered to the hungry bishop by Satan in disguise. Cranmere Pool from which seven of Devon's loveliest rivers have their source, and Widger's Cross are within walking distance. Bridestowe is also the nearest station to Black Tor, 1646 feet, Broad Tor 1511 feet, Chat Tor 1750 feet, Danagoat Tor 1845 feet, Ger Tor 1250 feet, Hare Tor 1744 feet, Kneeset Little 1694 feet, Great Links Tor 1908 feet, Great Nodden Tor 1430 feet, Sharp Tor 1701 feet and Woodcock Hill 1846 feet.

Lydford was popular on account of its ancient castle, the famous Lydford Gorge and for access to Bray Tor and Hare Tor. Lydford was inevitably the subject of considerable attention on the part of Southern Railway publicists. *Devon and Cornish Days*, E P Leigh Bennett, *Lets Get Out Here*, S P B Mais, and the annual publication of *Hints for Holidays* all featured Lydford's various attractions.

Looking south westward to the coast, Plymouth offered history plus dramatic land and sea escapes. It also enjoyed regular through corridor express services from Waterloo, Brighton, Portsmouth and Southampton, an asset stressed in the Company's work, *Winter Holidays in Southern England*, 1929 edition. Plymouth's waterfront had many moods and guises. From the restless energy of shipping in the Sound, to Old Plymouth with its Mayflower memories and Barbican atmosphere of long ago, there was something for everyone. *Hints for Holidays*, the Southern Railway handbook on tourism set out the attractions. The following is from the 1938 edition:

The Hoe has been described as the finest promenade in Europe and, indeed, it is difficult to imagine one more magnificent. It offers glorious views of Plymouth Sound, with the cliffs of Staddon on the east, the wonderful woods of Mount Edgcumbe on the west, away in the distance the thin line of the Breakwater, over a mile long, and in the foreground the picturesque stronghold of Drake's Island. At night the flashing of Eddystone Lighthouse, fifteen miles distant can be discerned, and on one part of the Hoe stands Smeaton's original lighthouse, which once stood at Eddystone.

Visitors to Plymouth never seem to tire of the ceaseless activity of the shipping in the Sound, and from the heights of the Citadel, towering above the Hoe, they obtain a panoramic view of the Hamonaze, where lie anchored mighty battleships and trim destroyers, their grim sternness relieved by the white wings of yachts and the puffs of smoke from the little pleasure steamers threading their way through the estuary of the Tamar to the idyllic riverside retreats beyond.

The Promenade Pier, opened in 1884, and the smaller stone built West Hoe Pier catered for river and sea trips, the Promenade Pier offering the traditional entertainments and facilities. The Pavillion accommodated some 2000 people and was open to various uses such as for concerts and roller-skating. Nearby was the new swimming baths opened in 193?, this was flood-lit at night by an underwater lighting scene and was open until 11pm. Sea bathing and the pleasures of the beach were also popular at Jennycliffe Bay and Bovisand. Again, as *Hints for Holidays* was glad to record:

Ideal picnic spots are plentiful around Plymouth, and on a fine day numerous happy parties can be seen leaving Turnchapel, 15 minutes by rail from Friary station, wending their way by devious routes to Jennycliffe and Bovisand, popular local holiday rendezvous.

A holiday excursion could be enjoyed on the Turnchapel branch as the line gave access to Jennycliffe and Bovisand, popular local attractions. Trains left from Friary and here an 02 No. 30207 is seen propelling its two coach push and pull set, the 9.03am Turnchapel-Friary, away from Lucas Terrace Halt, 21 August 1951.

N. Sprinks

Left: Dartmoor: Land of Romance, LSWR, 1915

Amongst the many boat trips available, that following the River Tamar to Calstock and Morwelham was particularly popular. Calstock, in what the Southern Railway called 'The Land of Fruit and Honey', was the exchange point for the joint rail and river excursions, passengers being persuaded to sample the district's famous strawberries and cream during the season.

The Tamar Valley and combined rail and river excursion were always popular. When the PDSWJR first opened in June 1890 the outstanding natural beauty of the line and its potential for tourism was acknowledged. The line was not only beautiful in terms of its landscape; it was diverse. On the lower reaches alongside the Tamar and across the Tavy Viaduct there were spectacular river views, whilst between Bere Ferrers and Bere Alston there were many examples of what the LSWR described as 'picturesque foregrounds of cherry orchards and strawberry fields'. By taking the Callington branch train at Bere Alston one was carried across the Tamar on the graceful Calstock Viaduct, thence into Cornwall with its widespread evidence of former tin and copper mine workings and the profusion of fruit fields bearing witness to a thriving market gardening industry. Kit Hill, between Gunnislake and Callington, the terminus, offered a vast panorama southward down the Tamar to Plymouth, westward to Caradon Hill and Cornwall and, eastward to Dartmoor.

In October 1936 the Southern Railway magazine carried an article on a 'Sight-Seeing Special from Exeter to Bere Alston', one of its many conducted Rail Tours, this one being on 2 August that year:

Unlike the majority of SR conducted tours which include a visit to some place of historic interest, this trip was entirely concerned with scenery. But what scenery! All the usual facilities were provided – comfortable open coaches with plenty of window space, itineraries describing places passed en-route, guides to point out objects of interest, a restaurant car where meals or light refreshments could be obtained and special slow timing to enable passengers to enjoy the scenery to the full.

We left Exeter Central at 12.38pm and proceeded along the valleys of the Exe and Creedy. Once past Yeoford strangers to the district began to look out eagerly for their first glimpse of the tors of Dartmoor, and as we steamed over Meldon Viaduct there was quite a rush to one side of the coaches to enjoy the close view of the Moor, with majestic Yes Tor looming up in the background. Later, by way of contrast came the magnificent wooded slopes of the Tavy Valley and the first glimpse of the Tamar with the woodswept heights of Cornwall beyond.

Leaving the train at Bere Alston we walked down through fields and lovely woods to the bank of the Tamar where the 'Western Belle' took us aboard conveying us up the winding river, beneath the shadow of Morwell Rocks to Weirhead, the highest navigable point. Then we came back down the broad sheet of water, with Devon on our left hand and Cornwall on our right, beneath the graceful viaduct which carries the Bere Alston to Calstock line, past picturesque villages, stately English homes and miles of wooded heights to Brunel's great bridge at Saltash. Then another change of scene – the outskirts of Plymouth, the great Naval Dockyard at Devonport, warships in the Hamonaze and a run through Plymouth Sound. We landed at Phoenix Wharf and spent a leisurely half-hour on the famous Hoe.

The train returned to Exeter Central via the Great Western line, leaving Plymouth at 8.10pm and arriving back at 10.32pm. Ten hours of travel and entertainment was offered for a fare of 5s. 6d. The Southern's reputation was enhanced by this, the excursion finding favour in the conclusion:

Small wonder that passengers announced their intention of coming again and bringing their families.

Padstow harbour during the 1920s. Like Port Isaac, Padstow was the source of an extensive fish traffic for the railway whilst its old-world appeal, river location and extensive beaches, locally, made it another prime Atlantic Coast resort. It was also the Southern's farthest outpost from Waterloo.
Cornwall Local Studies Library

North Cornwall, like Dartmoor and the Tamar Valley, proved to be a valuable possession for LSWR and Southern Railway interests in terms of the tourist trade. Padsow, Port Isaac, Tintagel and Boscastle, Bude and Bodmin Moor offered the excitement of historic landscape and outstanding natural beauty, combined with an easy access by rail.

Prior to World War One, the LSWR published its handbook on North Cornwall, *By the Cornish Sea and Moors; Holidays in King Arthur's Land*. S P B Mais wrote *My Finest Holiday*, a descriptive account of North Cornwall, published by the Southern Railway in 1927. In this work he emphasised the standards of service attained by the Southern:

All that modern engineering ingenuity can do to make fast railway travel pleasant and comfortable has been done. Long corridor coaches, luxuriantly appointed, mounted on wonderfully smooth running bogies; little shaded lights over each seat; clean and up to date washing and lavatory accommodation, comfortable restaurant cars with inexpensive meals efficiently served and the whole train hauled at express speed by a monitor green locomotive of *Lord Nelson* or *King Arthur* class – these are the contributions of an enterprising railway management to your holiday pleasure.

Mais also wrote the famous *Atlantic Coast Express* extolling the virtues of the Southern Railway and the magic and splendour of North Cornwall's landscape. His further publication also backed by the Southern Railway, *Lets Get Out Here* included details of several walks in the Padstow district, making use of the North Cornwall line as access.

The Homeland Handbook portrayed Padstow in exotic terms giving it another dimension in terms of time and place, surely with the particular approval of the Southern Railway anxious to make an impact in the Holidays at Home initiative:

After quitting the train we find that approach to the town from the station a remarkable one. We walk along the stony track by the line which is usually cumbered with trucks; between us and the river are sheds heaped with boxes, barrels and baskets, either containing fish or intended for fish, or just emptied of fish. The notion seizes us that we are not on British ground at all but have reached some small continental seaport and are humbly progressing towards the Custom House. The fact that we do pass the Custom House adds to the impression. Then we emerge upon the North Quay. The scene at high-tide is pretty enough; small vessels of different builds sway against one another; there is some desultory loading and unloading going on; idlers loiter about enjoying the aspect of other people's activity, and under the hill little low buildings of a more or less maritime character are clustered together ...

Narrow streets run interlaced by yet narrower ones, by and by we realise we have seen the whole of Padstow, assuredly, one of the quaintest, oddest little towns in all the kingdom.

" ATLANTIC COAST EXPRESS "

Corridor Restaurant Car Trains will run as under:

DOWN		Up to and including JULY 9th, 1927	From JULY 11th to SEPT. 24th, 1927, inclusive	
		Every Weekday	Sats. only	Every Weekday (Except Sats.)
		a.m.	a.m.	a.m.
LONDON (Waterloo)	dep.	11 0	10 25	11 10
		p.m.	p.m.	p.m.
BUDE	arr.	4 57	3 37	4 42
LAUNCESTON ...	arr.	4 41	3 15	4 20
CAMELFORD ... (For Boscastle and Tintagel)	arr.	5 18	3 53	4 58
PORT ISAAC ROAD	arr.	5 33	4 10	5 16
WADEBRIDGE ...	arr.	5 46	4 22	5 28
PADSTOW	arr.	5 59	4 35	5 41

UP		Up to and including JULY 9th, 1927	From JULY 11th to SEPT. 24th, 1927, inclusive
		a.m.	a.m.
PADSTOW	dep.	8 35	10 0
WADEBRIDGE ...	dep.	8 47	10 12
PORT ISAAC ROAD	dep.	9 6	10 29
CAMELFORD ...	dep.	9 24	10 47
LAUNCESTON ...	dep.	10 1	11 21
BUDE	dep.	9 45	10 58
		p.m.	p.m.
LONDON (Waterloo)	arr.	4 0	5 1

Seats can be reserved on trains at 1/- per seat. For full train service throughout the day and times at other North Cornwall stations see Time Tables at S. R. Stations.

Going to TINTAGEL?

Travel by the "Atlantic Coast Express" to

CAMELFORD

(thence by Motor Omnibus).

CORRIDOR RESTAURANT-CAR EXPRESSES

From LONDON (Waterloo) every Week-day, 6th July to 19th September, 1931, inclusive. Seats reserved in Compartments.

To TINTAGEL.

Atlantic Coast Exp. Sats. only. a.m.	R. Car London to Halwill	Atlantic Coast Exp. Not Sats. a.m.	R. Car Lon. t Ex. (Q. St.)							R. Car Lon. to Ex. (Q. St.) a.m.		R. Car Lon. to Ex. (Q. St.) p.m.		R. Car Lon. to Ex. (Q. St.) Sats. only. p.m.	
10 24		10 40		LONDON (Waterloo	dep.	"		11 0		12 40		3 0	
noon. 12 0		p.m. 12 14		SALISBURY	"			12 34		2 34		4 34	
1 45		2 10		EXETER -	"			2 28		4 49		6 38	
3 59		4 18		CAMELFORD	arr			5 24		7 32		9 18	
4A30		4A48		TINTAGEL	"			5 A50		8A10		—	

From TINTAGEL.

R. Car Exeter (Queen St.) to London a.m.		Atlantic Coast Ex. R. Car Exeter (Q. St.) to Lon. fromHal. on Sats. a.m.		TINTAGEL - dep				R. Car Exeter (Queen St.) to London. p.m.		R. Car Exeter (Queen St.) to London p.m.	
8A55		9A55		TINTAGEL - dep				12 55		—	
9 24		10 23		CAMELFORD - "				1B27		3 6	
p.m. 12 30		p.m. 12 44		EXETER - "				4 28		5 53	
2 14		2 40		SALISBURY - "				6 37		8 3	
3 46		4 13		LONDON - arr				8 41		10 6	
				(Waterloo)							

A—By Southern National Motor Omnibus.   B—Change at Okehampton.

CHEAP RETURN TICKETS from LONDON to CAMELFORD

TOURIST (May—Oct.)	HOLIDAY (On various days during the Summer)	WEEK-END (Friday—Tuesday)
54/6	39/9	39/9

Take a 7-DAY "HOLIDAY SEASON"

obtainable on demand any day during the Summer at any Station shown and available for seven days, including date of issue, at all Stations between Padstow, Wadebridge, Bodmin, Camelford, Launceston, Halwill and Bude.

TRAVEL WHEN— WHERE—and AS OFTEN as you like   **10/6** 3rd Cl.   **Children under 14 HALF-PRICE**   **Programmes at S.R. Stations**

CHEAP DAY TICKETS from CAMELFORD

On Week-days, as under:—

Launceston ...	2/6	Port Isaac Road ... 1/-
Padstow	2/6	Wadebridge 2/-

For full details of Train Services, Cheap Tickets, etc., see announcements at local S.R. Stations, or communicate direct with the Divisional Superintendent, Queen Street Station, Exeter.

SOUTHERN RAILWAY

Quickest Way to Sunshine.

Tintagel Castle, the famed Camelot of Arthurian legend. Described in *Hints For Holidays* as "one of the showpieces of England", and in the Southern's *Devon and Cornish Days* (1935) as "a colony of contentment with its clear, green seas, its coves, and caves and its cream". Camelford was the station for Tintagel. *Cornwall Local Studies Library*

Camelford was the railway gateway to Boscastle and Tintagel on the coast and to Bodmin Moor inland. Tourism was recognised as being of great potential when the North Cornwall line first opened there in August 1893. *The Cornish and Devon Post* reported:

The People of Camelford have just cut or are cutting a new carriage road to and round Roughtor, the most come-at-able and easily surmounted of the tors, and with the increasing recommendation of the medical faculty for moorland air the future before the town is far more hopeful. Tintagel and Boscastle to and from which conveyances run daily, while to Otterham, the station above, as many as 500 excursionists were brought from Exeter and Plymouth on Whit Monday.

Southern Railway promotional work showered praise on Tintagel leaving no room for doubt as to its appeal:

No photograph can do justice to the beauty of Tintagel – it is one of the showpieces of England. Unlike most beauty spots, it is far and away too lovely for the camera to capture its charm, especially when the summer sun creates its lights and shadows in the green valley and the gorse-clad and smooth-turfed castle mounds from backcloths for the flashing white of hundreds of seagulls. It is full of poetic and legendary interest.

This was Tintagel according to *Hints For Holidays*. Whilst also acclaiming its mystical qualities, its distinction from many other beauty spots, E P Leigh-Bennett in *Devon and Cornish Days* suggested a more relaxed atmosphere and a theme that was definitive of Southern Railway promotional work, namely, the decisive contrast between work and play; leisure and the routine of daily life:

Spattered upon the hillsides are the white cottages and the little hotels, so favoured by the holiday folk. It is a colony of contentment. The Tintagel coast could not be otherwise, with its green, clear seas, its coves and caves – and its cream. We are so beautifully far away, too, from all the thoughts of work, and duties, turmoil and office trivialities. We live so completely and perpetually the best sort of seaside life ....

Port Isaac offered tourists the experience of the traditional fishing village. In its depiction of the Cornish fishing community *The Homeland Handbook* drew upon the character, imagery and associations expected, much as the GWR had done for the likes of Looe, Newlyn or St Ives:

It is very steep, the houses jumbled together on the hillside, the windows of one overlooking the chimneys of those below. In and out among these houses wind little alleys and footpaths until we realise that there is a great deal more of the town than at first sight might be supposed. One especially picturesque corner is known as Temple Bar. We reach the shore, accompanied by the local brook running into the sea. There is a wide beach, hemmed in with cliffs that are hollowed into deep caverns. There are jumbles of lobster pots, boats pulled up on the shore, and the stir of comings and goings of the fishing town: besides the appearance on the hillside of pleasant looking houses affording the universal accommodation for visitors. The herring cellars, now disused are a special feature here and at Porth Gaverne – black,

L.&S.W.R.

(LONDON & SOUTH WESTERN RAILWAY.)

The Express Route

BETWEEN

LONDON (Waterloo Station)

AND THE

West of England.

> UP-TO-DATE CORRIDOR CARRIAGES
> IN THE PRINCIPAL SERVICES,
> — ALSO —
> BREAKFAST, LUNCHEON AND DINING CARS,
> To which Passengers travelling any class
> have access without extra charge, except
> cost of meals.

NORTH CORNWALL.

BUDE. 5 HOURS
ONLY FROM
LONDON.

By Direct Corridor Expresses.

(FROM WATERLOO STATION.)

Cheap Fares.	1st.	2nd.	3rd.	CIRCULAR TOUR
TOURIST*	66/6	41/6	35/9	"RAIL AND COACH" TRIPS.
WEEK END	50/9	31/9	25/6	INCLUDING
EXCURSION+	—	—	22/-	BUDE AND NORTH CORNWALL.

(*Issued during Summer Months only.)

CHEAP TICKETS BETWEEN BUDE

and principal surrounding

Places of Interest

IN

DEVON & CORNWALL.

THROUGH TICKETS TO BUDE

from principal towns in the

MIDLANDS & NORTH OF ENGLAND.

Ask for tickets

Via L. & S. W. R.

For full particulars of Train Service, Cheap Tickets, etc., apply to Mr. HENRY HOLMES, Superintendent of the Line, Waterloo Station, London, S.E.

H. A. WALKER, GENERAL MANAGER.

VIEW OF GARDENS AND BEACH FROM GRENVILLE HOTEL, BUDE   4

15084. Bathing Pool. Bude.

WIDEMOUTH BAY. BUDE

moist places where in former years the fish were stored after a large haul until they could be despatched by boat to other places or salted in barrels. The coming of the railway and the possibility of keeping fish in salt water tanks on the vessels has now rendered the old cellars unnecessary.

In its coverage of Bude, *Hints for Holidays* asserted that three kinds of holidaymakers are happy at Bude:

Those who are always active and on the move; those who ask for little else than a deck chair and a safe spot for the children to play in; and those who desire above everything unspoiled scenery of rare beauty.

E P Leigh-Bennett wrote:

You can have anything you want here except the Pier and Bandstand type of holiday. Bude is a place of great character. It bears no resemblance to any other seaside resort.

Bude was famous for its surf bathing:

Over acres of rich sand the long rollers of the Atlantic break in endless succession ... The breakers of Bude are a glorious spectacle to the swimmer and non swimmer alike. Then there are golf, tennis, bowls, badminton, croquet, fishing, boating on the canal and other pursuits for the sporting and energetic.

To indicate its distinctive character, Bude offered not the conventional promenade but, instead, Summerleaze Downs – a rising area of downland, 'purple with thyme' overlooking the main beach. 'It is here,' wrote *Hints For Holidays* 'that visitors gather to contemplate the magnificent Atlantic sunsets for which North Cornwall is renowned'. Finally, the 1938 edition of *Hints For Holidays* reminded readers that Bude also possessed 'a modern luxury picture theatre which specialises in matinees for unsettled afternoons'. Whilst the Southern Railway could not guarantee the weather, Bude, it seems, could offer the best of modern distractions.

The impact of tourism and good communications, through the railway, helped both Padstow and Bude to show useful growth and development, between the two World Wars and during the immediate post-war period. Between 1931 and 1939 Bude and Stratton Urban District grew by 9.2 per cent; Padstow by 7.4 per cent. Camelford and Launceston's large Rural districts, by contrast, suffered a fall of 6.8 per cent and 8.9 per cent respectively. Elsewhere in the county only Newquay and Looe, both established in tourism showed any comparable progress. LSWR and Southern Railway enterprise had played its part in helping to develop and sustain North Cornwall's economy through the promotion of tourism, increasingly the county's principal source of income.

Opposite:

Top: Estuary and beach at Bude as seen from the Grenville Hotel. It is a portrait of another, past, era of holiday-making, resonant of the *Atlantic Coast Express*, and, equally, of the numerous Half-Day Excursions to Bude from many other towns and cities served by the Southern Railway.

Middle: The bathing pool at Bude beach, a popular attraction given mention in the Southern's *Hints For Holidays* series. "Constructed in the natural rock formation . . . it is refreshed at high tide". Bude employed official lifeguards to ensure safe beaches.

Bottom: Widemouth Bay, three miles south of Bude, the definitive Atlantic Coast scenery and the inspiration for several Southern Railway promotional posters. *Hints For Holidays,* 1939, noted that Widemouth was "fast becoming a bungalow garden city."

Left Panel

LONDON AND SOUTH-WESTERN RAILWAY.

OPENING

OF THE

NEW LINE

FROM HALWILL JUNCTION TO LAUNCESTON.

ON 21ST JULY, 1886,

THE LONDON AND SOUTH-WESTERN RAILWAY COMPANY'S NEW LINE FROM HALWILL JUNCTION TO LAUNCESTON will be OPENED for Passengers and Goods Traffic. Passenger Trains will run between Halwill Junction and Launceston on every week day as under, and the train service between Okehampton and Holsworthy will be altered as shewn below.

N.B.—The up North Cornwall Coach will connect at Launceston with the 2.50. p.m. train from Launceston, and will return from Launceston at 4.15. p.m. after the arrival of the 9.0 a.m. Fast Train from Waterloo.

[UP TRAINS timetable — week days — stations listed: LAUNCESTON (dep), Tower Hill, Ashwater, Halwill Junction (arr), Bude (by Coach) (dep), HOLSWORTHY, Dunsland Cross, Hatherleigh Junction, ..., Okehampton (dep), Tavistock, Plymouth (North Road), Devonport, Okehampton (dep), Yeoford, Yeoford, Barnstaple, Ilfracombe, Bideford, EXETER (arr), Yeovil, Templecombe, Bournemouth, Bath (for Midland Line), Bristol (St. Philips), Salisbury, Southampton, Portsmouth, LONDON (Waterloo station) — timetable figures largely illegible]

* Bristol (Temple Mead.)

[DOWN TRAINS timetable — week days — stations listed: LONDON (Waterloo station) (dep), Portsmouth, Southampton, Salisbury, Bristol (St. Philip's), Bath, Bournemouth, Templecombe, Yeovil, EXETER, Bideford, Ilfracombe, Barnstaple, Yeoford, Yeoford, Okehampton (arr), Okehampton (dep), Devonport, Plymouth (North Road), Tavistock, Okehampton (arr), Okehampton (dep), Ashbury, Halwill Junction, Halwill Junction (dep), Dunsland Cross, HOLSWORTHY, Bude (by coach), Halwill Junction (dep), Ashwater, Tower Hill, LAUNCESTON — timetable figures largely illegible]

All these trains are first, second and third-class. No Sunday trains.

A Leave Launceston by North Cornwall Coach for Camelford, Wadebridge, and Padstow every week day and St. Columb and Newquay on Mondays, Wednesdays, and Fridays, at 4.15 p.m. after arrival of train due at Launceston at 4.0 p.m.

B Leave Newquay 8.0 a.m., St. Columb 9.15 a.m. on Tuesday, Thursdays and Saturdays, and Padstow 9.15 a.m. Wednesdays 10.49 a.m. and Camelford 12.15 p.m. on every week day by North Cornwall Coach to connect with 2.50 p.m. train from Launceston.

The train service between Launceston and Holsworthy on week days will be as follows:—

[Additional timetable — stations: LAUNCESTON (dep), Tower Hill, Ashwater, Halwill Junction (arr/dep see C), Dunsland Cross, HOLSWORTHY (arr), HOLSWORTHY (dep), Dunsland Cross, Halwill Junction (arr/dep see C), Ashwater, Tower Hill, LAUNCESTON — figures largely illegible]

C Change trains at Halwill Junction.

CHAS. SCOTTER, General Manager.

Right Panel

TUESDAY AND WEDNESDAY, 20TH AND 21ST JULY.

OPENING

OF THE

NORTH CORNWALL RAILWAY

From Halwell to

LAUNCESTON

GREAT ATTRACTIONS!

STEEPLECHASES!

ATHLETIC SPORTS!

FANCY FAIR!

ILLUMINATIONS, DECORATIONS, GORGEOUS PROCESSIONS, AND OTHER ATTRACTIONS.

Public Notices.

OPENING OF THE NORTH CORNWALL RAILWAY TO LAUNCESTON.

In aid of the Funds of the New Town Hall, a

GRAND FANCY DRESS

BALL

will be held on Tuesday, the 20th, 1886, in a specially-prepared Marquee, to be erected in the Castle Green.

Fancy costumes or evening dress must be worn.

The Devon Engineer Volunteer Band will attend.

Dancing to commence at Ten p.m.

Tickets, if applied for on or before the 17th July, 5s. each (Refreshments included), wine extra; after that date, 7s. 6d.

Tickets may be obtained from either of the following members of the Ball Committee:—

C. R. G. GRYLLS, Heightleigh, Launceston.

W. I. F. BRAND, Launceston.

C. C. JAMES, St. Leonards, Launceston.

C. H. PETER, Northenhaye, Launceston.

Dated Guildhall, 2nd July, 1886.

Chapter Five
THE NORTH CORNWALL RAILWAY

Falmouth was the ultimate prize for LSWR interests with their plans to develop westward. According to company supporters they had every hope of fulfilling their ambition, or, as they put it:

> They would not rest content until they could dip their hands in Falmouth harbour.

Being the world's third largest natural harbour, Falmouth had its attractions and the Cornwall Central Railway, fought for its central, standard gauge line in the Parliamentary battles of the mid 1840s. It was defeated and Brunel's broad gauge coastal route held sway but the project would not go away and reappeared in different guises throughout the mid and later nineteenth century.

One such example was the Launceston, Bodmin and Wadebridge Railway's scheme with a plan for a standard gauge line to Truro, then Falmouth and Penzance. It was taken seriously by the local press, the *Royal Cornwall Gazette* referring to it as:

> . . . the most important railway scheme that has been brought forward in Cornwall since the severe costly battle of the broad and narrow gauges.

Supporters pointed out that the southern coastal districts served by the broad gauge Cornwall Railway had flourished since 1859; they also pointed to large tracts of central and north Cornwall that needed urgent assistance in the form of a reliable railway. The case seemed clear:

> It must be admitted that an extensive and important area in northern and central parts of the county is, so to speak, literally shut out of this world. Here is a rich mineral and agricultural district, and a large and growing population call loudly for a share of the benefits which railways afford and it is only fair that no stumbling blocks should be thrown in the way. We cannot expect that an enterprising people will forever sit down quietly without ever participating with their neighbours in the privileges which distinguish this progressive age; nor will any intelligent person contend that such a state of things is desirable. Rather will he boldly admit that they are entitled to every aid we can render them . . .

Aid, was, of course, the LSWR who had earlier, in 1845, purchased the Bodmin and Wadebridge Railway thereby claiming their stake in developments locally. The Bodmin and Wadebridge line was to be a vital element in the newly projected railway route through the country:

> We see a proof of new life and vigour consequent on the obtaining the bill for the narrow gauge from Launceston to the centre of the county last year, in the fact that the South Western solicitors have given notice of an application to Parliament relative to such improvements on the Bodmin and Wadebridge line as will make it one of the best locomotive lines in England.

Sealing the identity of the LSWR with progress and opportunity, it was further stressed that the South-Western:

> . . . are as well aware as we who live in the county that an undertaking which will be the means of forming a complete line of narrow gauge railway from the west of Cornwall to London, Portsmouth and other important places and which will materially develop not only the northern central and western portions of our county but also northern and mid Devon is one in the welfare of which they are largely interested.

Proceeding to details of the route, these were as follows:

> The main line will commence by a junction with the Ruthern Bridge branch of the Bodmin and Wadebridge Railway and proceed in a westerly direction passing a little to the north of Withiel and St Wenn, until within a mile and a half of St Columb. It will then take a turn to the northwards and passing about half a mile north-east of St Columb at which point a convenient station will be situated, cross under the Newquay railway at Halewoon, where it will begin a short branch line to form a junction with the railway just mentioned. It will then proceed on the western side of Indian Queens, on the south of St Enoder and on the north of St Michael, running down the Kenwyn Valley by means of Idless and under Kenwyn near St Mary's burial ground and across the valley to the Truro station where it will form a junction with the Cornwall and West Cornwall Railways.

The company gained its power to build the new line through an Act of 1865. St Columb celebrated, the local Rifle Brigade being turned out in full dress uniform, the church bells being rung at length and barrels of ale were distributed. This, however, was as far as things went; in terms of actual construction it was no more successful than the earlier schemes of 1836 and 1845, or of the later attempts in 1875/1876 on the part of the Cornwall Minerals and Bodmin and Wadebridge Junction Railway despite the latter gaining its powers.

Other than in its ownership of the Bodmin and Wadebridge Railway, the LSWR finally secured a realistic working identity within Cornwall from the summer of 1882. On 18 August that year, the North Cornwall Railway was incorporated, thereafter being opened in stages from Halwill Junction in West Devon to Padstow on the North Cornish coast. Construction, overall, took some fifteen years, the first section being from Halwill to Launceston, opening officially on 20 July 1886 and to general traffic the following day. The first sod was cut on 20 June 1884 at Halwill, the Chairman of the Board of Directors, Mr. J Tremayne and the local MP Mr. J W Harris, sharing the honours. Two years of varyingly heavy construction – there were extensive embankments and cuttings, but no tunnels or viaducts – saw completion into the ancient, historic Cornish border town. Acting for the Board of Trade, Colonel Rich inspected the 13 3/4 miles of line on Tuesday 13 July. Two locomotives and two coaches made up the inspection train, the contractors, Messrs Currie, Reeve and Company providing luncheon for the inspection party at Tower Hill station.

Mid morning activity at Halwill. 'West Country' Class No. 34107 *Blandford Forum* arrives with the 8.30am Padstow-Waterloo whilst N class 2-6-0 No. 31843 waits with the 9.56am Okehampton-Padstow. The pathway beyond the main platform led to the Torrington bay where Ivatt 2-6-2T, No. 41312 waits with the 10.38am for Torrington. As the photograph shows and the station nameboard announces, Halwill was station for Beaworthy and junction for Bude, North Cornwall and Torrington lines! 25 September 1962.

R. C. Riley

Morning activity at Halwill Junction. E1/R 0-6-2T, No. 32610 approaches its bay platform with the 8.52am train from Torrington; M7 0-4-4T, No. 30320 is engaged in shunting through coaches from Bude, prior to attaching them to an eastbound service from Padstow. 22 August 1951.

Neil Sprinks

T9 No. 30715 near Ashwater with a Padstow train. For much of the route between Halwill Junction and the Cornish border this line followed the charming River Carey. *M. Esau*

Two intermediate stations, Ashwater, 5 miles, and Tower Hill, 8½ miles, were provided. Both served isolated, rural communities, the latter being the subject of considerable dispute as to its appropriateness and siting. Boldford was thought by many to be a better proposition. Ashwater and Tower Hill were virtually identical, comprising a ticket office, large waiting room, the folding glazed doors and an adjoining station-master's house, these being on the 'up' platform. A spacious waiting room was also available on the 'down' platform, both platform faces being of asphalt. The buildings were of local blue stone with white stone facings and were described at the time as being of a 'semi gothic style, presenting a very picturesque appearance'.

Launceston station was the most important being 'very much larger and fitted with every convenience ...it left nothing to be desired'. Being sited on low ground, the station site required considerable infilling, moreover the site generally needed clearance with several houses being demolished in the process. A large station house, goods shed, locomotive shed and turntable completed facilities. The stations were the work of Messrs Bull and Son of Southampton.

The town did not stint of the celebrations for the new line. Streets were decorated with flowers, evergreens, banners and commemorative arches proclaiming 'Success To The North Cornwall Railway'. Illuminations focussed on the castle and firework displays added to the sense of occasion. A special train from Exeter brought the Chairman of the North Cornwall Railway and certain of its directors, together with Mr C Scotter, General Manager of the LSWR and many more officials linked with the railway. This arrived at 10.30 to 'the ringing of

church bells and great rejoicing' and was formally welcomed by the Mayor and Corporation. At 10.50 the entire entourage left for a commemorative journey to Halwill, this being marked en-route by fog signals and cheers from onlookers at the lineside. On their return to Launceston at 12.30 some 60 invited guests enjoyed an official luncheon. Amongst the speeches, the Mayor proposed the toast of the day: 'Success to the North Cornwall Railway'. He noted:

> The new line will prove to both the Company and the town of Launceston, a great success and source of profit. He thought there was no doubt of this when they knew how much easier their produce would be got off and with how much greater ease people would be able to visit the natural beauties of the neighbourhood, while the line would have the advantage of bringing Launceston into closer association with the great centres of civilisation.

The principal features of the line from Halwill were to be found in its embankments and cuttings. As mentioned, there were no tunnels or viaducts. Leaving Halwill's newly enlarged station on a northwesterly direction, the line quickly curved around southwestward to descend through the valley of the River Carey. A considerable sitting below Halwill provided large amounts of spoil for the nearby embankment – 'The Big Bank' – this being 40 feet high. Built on marshland, the embankment consumed vast quantities of rubble and was destabilised by a water-course which had to be diverted.

From Ashwater to Tower Hill the line passed though what was considered to be the most picturesque

'West Country' No. 34030 *Watersmeet* leaves Launceston with the 'up' *Atlantic Coast Express* on 22 August, 1964.   *P. Gray*

N Class 2-6-0 No. 31837 stands at Launceston with the fireman seen here taking on water. The train was the 3.13pm Padstow-Exeter. 2 May, 1961.
R. C. Riley

surroundings. In the words of the *Cornish and Devon Post*:

> The scenery maintains all its romantic character all the way from Ashwater to Tower Hill, a distance of about four miles passing through the lovely Virginstowe or Tileslow Woods where the stone was got for Launceston station and skirting the Carey all the way down until it crosses the Tamar.

Before crossing the Tamar the line again negotiated an impressive embankment over meadowland at Hele, some three miles from Launceston where the line crosses the River Carey for the final time on a masonry bridge of three arches. The cutting at Hele also gave trouble in construction as the sub-soil was extremely wet and unstable and there were several springs breaking into the works. A bed of faggots and furse was laid down in the cutting by way of foundation. To cross the Tamar the Company provided a girder bridge on granite piers, and having crossed that river, soon also crosses the River Kensey. The river and its surrounding marshland required attention in the form of a bridge, banking and drainage, the river being diverted and straightened in the process. Bridging the river was a masonry structure, 120 feet in length, with three arches of 28 feet and a substantial retaining wall. To the south of the line was the GWR branch from Tavistock, running westward from Lifton. A girder bridge carried the North Cornwall line over the GWR with the latter then running parallel to the south, and with the Kensey meadows to the north. The North Cornwall and GWR stations were alongside each other, the former being of a more elaborate, extensive nature. Approaching Launceston, passengers were given a splendid view of the motte and bailey castle and the landscape of the town, high on the hill above them to the south.

Extending westward beyond Launceston, the line opened to Tresmeer, eight miles distant, on 28 July 1892. Work did not begin until October 1890. 650 navvies found employment but the works were not considered heavy. The line again followed the Kensey Valley, this time, to Egloskerry. Although a station was provided there it was not completed in time for the opening of the line; Egloskerry eventually opened on 4 October 1892.

Having satisfied the Board of Trade inspection, the line opened to Tresmeer on Thursday 28 July, the occasion of the Launceston Agricultural Show. From Launceston to Egloskerry the gradient was 1 in 132 at its steepest but from Egloskerry on to Tresmeer the gradient stiffened to 1 in 74 as the line climbed westward. Although 28 July was the official opening day, the first train actually ran on Tuesday 26 July. That afternoon a special train conveyed all the requisite furniture for the station together with one or two local celebrities such as the vicar of Egloskerry who joined the train at the then incomplete station, 'in order to celebrate the event whereby Egloskerry comes within the sphere of civilisation'.

The next stage of the North Cornwall Railway was that of 9½ miles from Tresmeer to Camelford opening on Monday 14 August 1893. A holiday was declared for the town and the neighbouring district and the first train brought some 700 people by way of celebration. The main train of the day arrived at Camelford at 1.15pm being announced by fog signals on the line. It brought the directors of the North Cornwall Railway and

U1 Class No. 31904 seen here with an eastbound train from Padstow to Okehampton near Egloskerry.   *M. Esau*

West of Tresmeer Standard Class 4 2-6-4T No. 80041 heads two very different styles of coaching stock comprising the 3.10pm Padstow-Exeter on 22 August, 1964.
P. Gray

representatives of the LSWR. Colonel Hawker offered the customary address on the platform itself drawing upon the significance of historical tradition and the comparison and contrasts of past and present; time and place and the inevitable influence of the railway within the district':

It was a curious circumstance that on the very spot that they were assembled a great battle was fought between King Arthur and his nephew Modred and later on, between the Britons and Saxons. Today there was not the din of battle or the clash of arms, but they came there amid fields of waving corn and joyous shouts of peaceful people to bring the blessings of an advancing civilisation and culture; for a railway not only induced a better cultivation of the land but a rising civilisation and culture in the inhabitants of the district into which it came, because they would be drawn nearer to centres of culture and learning which would be within easy reach of the shores of Bude and Old Tintagel and the everlasting hills of Rough Tor and Brown Willy.

Specific and detailed reference to the railway as the direct agent of civilisation were a feature of all the ceremonies along the course of the line from Launceston to Padstow, marking out a definitively new era for the district.

1200 children from the neighbourhood were given buns and ginger beer together with a commemorative medal as a celebration of the events. The medal had the Cornish motto and shield 'One and All' on one side, and an inscription 'North Cornwall Railway Opened August 1893, Camelford, Boscastle and Tintagel, May We Prosper' on the other.

Heavy engineering and a long climb at 1 in 73 to the summit of the line west of Otterham defined this stage into Camelford. From Tresmeer, with its brick-built station the line swung northwestward to avoid negotiating a difficult valley and the high ground on the northwestern flank of Bodmin Moor. The substantial Treneglos embankment was required, 86 feet high, and following a curve to cross the valley. There had been plans to provide a viaduct here but a shortage of building stone and problems with foundations prevented this. The 'cut and fill' procedure was followed here using spoil from a major cutting beyond the embankment which required excavation to 60 feet.

Otterham station followed this being some 900 feet above sea level. The station was built in the same style as others on the line; here the material was stone and grey slate. Main buildings were on the 'up' side with a small yard gained from the 'down' side loop. From the summit west of Otterham, and further evidence of substantial cuttings as the line fringed Bodmin Moor, there was a descent at 1 in 80 for most of the way into Camelford.

In typical North Cornish landscape, this section of the line marking the summit, N Class No. 31859 brings the 1.00pm Padstow-Okehampton into Otterham on 22 August, 1964.

P. Gray

Camelford on 15 July, 1960. T9 No. 30719 stands at the down platform with a morning train from Okehampton – Camelford, as the station nameboard says, was the railway access for Boscastle and Tintagel, valuable assets for LSWR/Southern Railway publicity purposes.

R. C. Riley

Delabole, famed for its slate quarrying, was the next objective, this 2¹/₂ mile section of line being opened on Wednesday 18 October 1893. As with the previous extensions of the railway there were special trains and extensive celebrations, estimates put the number of people attending at between six and seven thousand. The company chairman paid tribute to the LSWR and to the landowners and the railway navvies themselves during the celebratory luncheon at the Cooperative Rooms. Lord Robartes, a principal landowner, was especially noted for his whole-hearted support for the line and for accommodating the company in every way over the question of land, access and accommodation. The navvies together with the local quarry men were given a free luncheon which eventually catered for over 1100. The North Cornwall chairman told his guests that there was a force of between five and six hundred navvies then employed on the section of line below Delabole and that he anticipated further celebrations within two years when the line reached into Wadebridge. In a further tribute he asserted: 'The spade of the navvy did more to advance the cause of humanity than the sword of the soldier'.

Whilst at Delabole for the occasion, the chairman and officials of LSWR took the opportunity to visit Padstow as the eventual objective for the railway and the source of an extensive tourist trade, and fish traffic.

Engineering works on the eleven mile section between Delabole and Wadebridge were not considered heavy, but there was a long descent mainly at 1 in 73 and 1 in 75 to Wadebridge at almost sea level. This section also included the North Cornwall's only tunnel, this being at Trelill, between Port Isaac Road and St Kew Highway. Trelill Tunnel was 352 yards and took its name from the local community. In contrast with the starker upland sections of the line above Port Isaac, the lower reaches of the line towards Wadebridge were considered charmingly rural, lush and fertile. On its final run into Wadebridge itself, the line crossed the Rivers Allen and the Camel, joining alongside the earlier Bodmin and Wadebridge Railway, the two lines running parallel giving the impression of a double track railway.

The two intermediate stations, Port Isaac Road and St Kew Highway, were both stone built structures with their main buildings on the 'up' side. At Port Isaac there was a goods shed and yard also on the 'up' side behind the platform and a signal box sited half-way along the 'up' platform. Port Isaac Road despite being some distance from the fishing port itself contributed a useful traffic in fish; the railway also opened up the community to tourism, for which there was great potential. St Kew Highway was situated immediately south of what became the A39 trunk road between Wadebridge and Bude. The station served a widespread rural area, St Kew to the northwest and St Mabyn to the south being the main villages. A small goods yard was provided on the 'up' side, likewise a signal box off the south end of the 'up' platform.

Delabole, rightly famous for its slate quarries, seems to be benefiting from a certain level of activity here on 15 July, 1960. T9 No. 30719 heads the 9.56am Okehampton-Padstow.

R. C. Riley

T9 No. 30718 near Port Isaac Road with an evening train for Okehampton. *M. Esau*

Waiting for the train at St Kew Highway. Preserved and much admired T9 No. 120 waits at the 'down' platform with an RCTS/PRC Railtour on 27 April, 1963 whilst a specially decorated N Class No. 31874 enters the station from Wadebridge.   *P. Gray*

Wadebridge welcomed the railway in June 1895. The town had welcomed two rail services prior to the North Cornwall. The Bodmin and Wadebridge, distinguished by being one of Britain's earliest railways, had opened in 1834; the GWR opened its service from Bodmin Road on its main line in September 1888. The arrival of the North Cornwall Company, however, was perceived as being the most significant of these developments for the town, with the reality of through services to Waterloo.

Colonel Yorke in the company of the District Superintendent, the District Engineer and various other officials of the North Cornwall Company, inspected the line from Delabole on Tuesday 28 May 1895. Following a thorough examination of Trelill Tunnel and the various bridges, embankments and cuttings Colonel Yorke expressed 'unqualified satisfaction'. A special inspection train comprising two large locomotives with tenders and two coaches made repeated runs over the bridges en-route and made careful inspection of the permanent way, with the result that 'not the slightest defect can be found'.

Although the line opened on Saturday 1 June the official celebration and opening was held over until 12 June to coincide with the Royal Cornwall Agricultural Show. The section from Delabole to Port Isaac was, in fact, complete for the August of the previous year but the LSWR, much to the disappointment of the community at Port Isaac, delayed the opening until the entire line to Wadebridge was complete.

Wadebridge was a joint station with staff from both companies employed. The main buildings were on the 'down' side, to the south; an island platform dealt with departures and 'up' services once the line was extended to Padstow. Also on the 'down' north side, close to the River Camel, was the locomotive shed and the turntable. The goods shed was on the 'up' side close to the main buildings and adjoining the platform.

A service of five trains in each direction brought Wadebridge into good contact with the outside world, and especially to those destinations served by the extensive LSWR network. Much was made of links with Waterloo, weekday departures from Wadebridge being given as at 7.00am, 9.15am, 10.20am, 1.15pm and 2.36pm. From Waterloo they were at 5.50am, 9.00am, 11.00am, 1.00pm and 3.00pm.

Wadebridge showing one of the steam motors from the early years of this century when the LSWR operated these services to and from Bodmin. Note the wooden footbridge in this view looking towards Padstow.   *Cornwall Local Studies Library*

Another view of Wadebridge in relatively more recent times. T9 No. 30719 waits to leave for Okehampton with the 3.15pm from Padstow on 15 May, 1960. A Western Region 'B' set can be seen on the opposite platform, for Bodmin.   *R. C. Riley*

U Class No. 31610 leaves Wadebridge on the North Cornwall line with the 1.00pm Padstow-Exeter, 1 August, 1958. The appearance of double track is suggested, but the other line was that to Bodmin North (SR) to Bodmin General (GWR) and to Bodmin Road on the GWR main line. It also gave access, of course, to Wenford Bridge for freight traffic.   *C. Hogg*

Not really part of the Southern's holiday image, but too good to miss! The Beattie LSW tanks Nos. 30585, 30586 and 30587 on shed at Wadebridge in June, 1962.
R. C. Riley

The Bodmin and Wadebridge route shared by Southern and GWR services was an outstanding experience of rural landscape – the woodland, river and fields offering much to enjoy. This view of a Southern service near Grogley, the 4.15pm Bodmin North-Padstow with 02 Class No. 30200 is typical of the line. 10 September, 1960.
P. Gray

The section of line between Wadebridge and Padstow offered superb views of the River Camel and the shoreline opposite. Here a T9, No. 30712, heads towards Wadebridge with a mixed train.
C. Hogg

A view from the footplate as T9 No. 30712 approaches Little Petherick Creek and its distinctive viaduct on 15 July 1960. The monument on Denis Hill marked the fiftieth anniversary of Queen Victoria's reign, in 1887. A substantial cutting carried the line through the side of this hill.
R. C. Riley

It took a further four years to complete the North Cornwall Railway. Thursday 23 March 1899 saw the arrival of the first trains to Padstow. The five mile section from Wadebridge ran along the south bank of the River Camel offering spectacular views across the water and seaward to Padstow itself. There were no problems of gradient, the main engineering features being the girder bridge at Little Petherick Creek and the two cuttings each side of the approach. The creek presented difficulties in terms of the accumulated mud and reports from Messrs Bell and Co in charge of construction detailed the need to drive down to 53 feet to fix the necessary foundations and also to put in a heavy concrete base. The bridge consisted of a three span girder section each of 133 feet and supported by cylinder section piers, eight feet in diameter. Height above water at high tide was 16 feet and 30 feet above the mud. Two major cuttings leading on to the bridge provided spoil for infilling at Dennis Cove between the bridge and Padstow station. An embankment replaced the creek. There were also heavy excavations at the station itself. Considerable work was required to cut ground back from the landslide rock face to give adequate land for the station site. On the sea side, land was reclaimed by infilling. In its riverbank site Padstow station – a single platform on the 'down' side – the yard and locomotive turntable occupied one of Britain's most dramatic landscape settings. Messrs Galbraith and Church were engineers to the line and Messrs Curry-Reeve were, again, the contractors. Colonel Yorke inspected the line on Tuesday 21 March.

To record the opening event on the opening day, a special train left Exeter at 9.30, calling at Launceston at 11.00am and Wadebridge at 12.10pm. Fog signals were put on the line at both Wadebridge and Padstow to welcome the train. The Padstow Artillery and the Delabole Brass Bands welcomed the official train with the inevitable rendition of 'See The Conquering Hero Comes'. 1000 children and adults were given a free trip to Wadebridge and such was the popularity and demand that a second service was run later in the day. A free meat tea was also provided, catering for 1000 people.

At 259 1/2 miles from Waterloo, Padstow became the furthest outpost on the London and South Western Railway. Well disposed to capitalise on the fishing industry and on tourism both the railway and the community generally looked forward to prosperity.

The Grouping brought all LSWR territory under the control of the Southern Railway. Publicity for North Cornwall as a holiday area was intensified and the West of England was given a new titled train, *The Atlantic Coast Express*. This multi-portioned train served all the major Southern holiday resorts in Devon and Cornwall. Introduced in July 1926, the *ACE* was the Southern's prestigious version of the rival Great Western's *Cornish Riviera Express*. Sir Herbert Walker, General Manager of the Southern Railway, anxious to enhance the imagery of the Southern's West of England service instigated a competition wherein staff members submitted possible names for the principal West of England working, the 11.00am from Waterloo. An employee from Torrington offered up *The Atlantic Coast Express*. Inspired by the landscape of North Cornwall and North Devon, although it also ran to Plymouth, the train was celebrated in S P B Mais' book of the same name published, of course, by the company itself. The first actual *Atlantic Coast Express* left Waterloo on 19 July 1926, hauled by 'King Arthur' Class 4-6-0 No E779 *Sir Colgrevance*. Until the post-war years and the introduction of Bulleid's Pacifics – the 'Merchant Navy' and 'West Country/Battle of Britain' classes, the *ACE* was normally handled by 4-6-0 'Lord Nelson' and 'King Arthur' classes east of Exeter, with Southern Railway 2-6-0 'N' class moguls taking charge generally west of Exeter. The standard of coaching stock was also much improved with the introduction of new Maunsell designed vehicles in 1926.

Train services to and from Padstow in the summers of 1914 and 1932 were as follows:

SUMMER SEASON 1914

ARRIVALS

9.41 am	dep	Launceston	8.17 am	
10.33 am	dep	Okehampton	8.14 am	July-Sept
12.21 pm	dep	Exeter Queen St	8.40 am	
3.45 pm	dep	Exeter Queen St	11.48 am	
5.06 pm	dep	Waterloo	11.00 am	*North Cornwall and Bude Express* 18 July-29 Sept
6.14 pm	dep	Exeter Queen St	2.36 pm	
8.27 pm	dep	Waterloo	1.00 pm	

DEPARTURES

6.45 am	arr	Waterloo	1.47 pm	
8.20 am	arr	Waterloo	3.17 pm	
10.55 pm	arr	Waterloo	5.17 pm	Luncheon Car from Padstow from 20 July
12.47 pm	arr	Waterloo	8.07 pm	
2.25 pm	arr	Waterloo	10.34 pm	
5.50 pm	arr	Exeter Queen St	9.27 pm	
8.00 pm	arr	Okehampton	10.33 pm	July-Sept

SUMMER SEASON 1932

ARRIVALS

9.01am	dep	Launceston	7.45am	
12.09pm	dep	Okehampton	10.00am	Not Fri/Sats 22 July-10 Sept.
12.14pm	dep	Okehampton	10.00am	23 July-10 Sept. Sats only
12.19pm	dep	Okehampton	10.00am	Fri only
3.36pm	dep	Okehampton	1.00pm	
4.57pm	dep	Waterloo	10.45am	Sats only 23 July-10 Sept
5.00pm	dep	Waterloo	10.35am	Not Sats 18 July-9 Sept
6.09pm	dep	Waterloo	11.00am	
7.03pm	dep	Exeter	3.52pm	Fri only 22 July-9 Sept
8.09pm	dep	Okehampton	5.52pm	Not Sat 23 July-10 Sept.
8.36pm	dep	Okehampton	6.27pm	Sats only 23 July-10 Sept.
9.13pm	dep	Waterloo	3.00pm	
(Camelford)				

DEPARTURES

7.39 (Launceston) arr Okehampton 8.38am				
8.35am	arr	Okehampton	11.09am	(Exeter Mon-Fri.18 July-9 Sept)
9.40am	arr	Waterloo	4.13pm	Not Sats. 18 July-9 Sept.
10.15am	arr	Waterloo	5.09pm	Fri only 22 July-9 Sept.
10.25am	arr	Waterloo	4.38pm	Sats only 23 July-10 Sept.
12.38pm	arr	Waterloo	8.41pm	
2.17pm	arr	Okehampton	4.44pm	
5.48pm	arr	Okehampton	8.29pm	

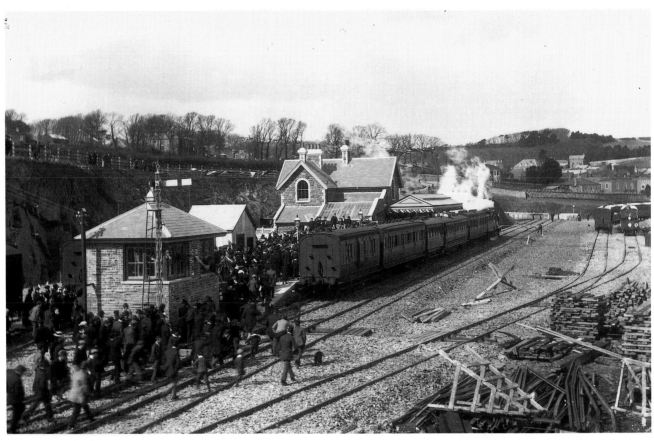

A famous view of the arrival of the first train at Padstow on Thursday, 23 March, 1899.   *Royal Institution of Cornwall*

T9 No. 30719 recorded at Padstow with the empty stock for the 3.13pm departure over the North Cornwall line.   *R. C. Riley*

North Cornwall and North Devon offered the quintessential experience of the Atlantic Coast, the equivalent, in imagery and intention of the 'Ocean Coast' ethos created by the Great Western. Tourism and the tourist traffic was one decisive growth area in the Thirties and the Southern Railway in particular did well from this traffic, its territory, overall, escaping the worst of the Depression years and showing a marked increase in population and affluence. The *Holidays with Pay Act* of 1938 increased the potential for tourism considerably but the real peak of railway tourist traffic came after 1945,

reaching its best years in the mid 1950s.

By this time, of course, the railways had been nationalised and the Southern Railway became the Southern Region, British Railways from 1 January 1948. The post war period also saw the introduction of Bulleid's 'West Country'/'Battle of Britain' Light Pacifics which, with their excellent power to weight ratio, enabled them to work through to Padstow, although this did not apply to the later rebuilt members of the class. An enlarged turntable was installed at Padstow in 1947 to cater for these locomotives.

Summer Saturday services to and from Padstow are given here for 1955:

ARRIVALS

7.42 am	– Waterloo	dep	12.35 am	16 July–10 Sept
9.27 am	– Waterloo	dep	1.15 am	Begins 3 Sept
9.27 am	– Waterloo	dep	1.25 am	Until 27 Aug
12.30 pm	– Okehampton	dep	10.15 am	
2.14 pm	– Waterloo	dep	7.33 am	
5.00 pm	– Waterloo *ACE*	dep	10.35 am	
6.22 pm	– Waterloo	dep	11.15 am	
7.58 pm	– Okehampton	dep	5.51 pm	

DEPARTURES

8.10 am (Wadebridge)	arr	Waterloo	3.04 pm	
8.30 am	arr	Waterloo	3.23 pm	
			16 July–27 Aug	
11.00 am *Atlantic Coast Express*				
	arr	Waterloo	5.24 pm	
1.00 pm	arr	Waterloo	8.25 pm	
3.15 pm	arr	Okehampton	5.47 pm	
6.00 pm	arr	Okehampton	8.29 pm	

Preserved T9 No. 120 at Padstow with a member of the crew recording the event. The RCTS/PRC Special was about to return to Exeter, 27 April, 1963.

P. Gray

'West Country' Class Light Pacific No. 34107 *Blandford Forum* heads the 'down' *Atlantic Coast Express* near Maddaford Moor Halt on 4 August, 1964. Maddaford Moor was a Southern Railway halt opened between Okehampton and Halwill Junction on 27 July, 1926. Dartmoor can be seen in the far distance, eastward.

P. Gray

A rarity for the North Cornwall line here as U Class 2-6-0 No. 31802 is seen with the 1.00pm from Padstow in open country near Maddaford Moor Halt. The train is made up from a very mixed stock and would invariably have been headed by an N or, earlier, a T9.

P. Gray

Under boundary changes introduced in 1950, all the former LSWR lines west of Exeter were transferred into the control of the Western Region, but outwardly there was little to show for it. In 1958 the Southern regained control and the Western Region took full control west of Salisbury. The following year saw the end for the *Atlantic Coast Express*. On 5 September 1964 'West Country' Pacific No.34015 'Exmouth' brought the very last *ACE* into Padstow. At the same time, the Southern's Salisbury-Exeter line lost its status as a main trunk route, the major West of England services being concentrated upon Paddington and future investment being devoted to the Berks and Hants route. Singling of the Salisbury-Exeter line began in 1966 together with widespread closures of West Country branch lines. British Railways, in April 1964, announced that the North Cornwall and Bude lines were losing £100,000 per year. Southern steam on the North Cornwall lines ceased in January 1965 and on 3 October 1966 the last train from Wadebridge to Halwill, no more than a single car 'Gloucester' unit, further strengthened by another single car at Launceston, brought the railway presence to an end.

Having celebrated the opening of the line and reported its business for eighty years, *The Cornish and Devon Post* had to duly record the closure of the North Cornwall and Bude lines. On Saturday 1 October 1966 the paper paid tribute to the railways of the district by including the following:

With the exception of the footholds at Okehampton, Wadebridge and for the time, at least, at Callington, the railway era comes to an end in this district tomorrow (Saturday) when the last trains will run over the Bude and North Cornwall lines.

The *Post* concluded:

We hazard the guess that the railway buildings will long remain to serve, as do the present smouldering mine-stacks, as a mute reminder of a very different past.

The 49 miles 67 chains comprising the North Cornwall Railway from Halwill to Padstow took some 17 years to complete, from its Act of Incorporation in August 1882 to its actual arrival at Padstow in March 1899. For the next 68 years Padstow played host to the railway. The bulk of the North Cornwall line, from Halwill to Wadebridge, closed on 3 October 1966, but a local service from the former GWR main line at Bodmin Road serving Bodmin General and Wadebridge to Padstow survived until 30 January 1967. During its relatively short life the North Cornwall Railway played a valuable part in serving the local community and contributed significantly in the creation of the later Southern Railway's 'Atlantic Coast' imagery, drawing extensively upon the history, traditions and magical quality of the North Cornwall landscape.

A Bude bound train about to cross over the A30 trunk road on the curve away from Meldon Junction. N Class No. 31853 is in charge of the 4.24pm Okehampton-Bude on 5 August, 1963.
P. Gray

Chapter Six
TO HOLSWORTHY AND BUDE

Monday 20 January 1879 was, according to the *Cornish and Devon Post*, 'The day of all days in the history of Holsworthy'. Under a leaden sky and a biting wind crowds estimated at between 10,000 and 14,000 turned out to welcome the railway. On the previous Saturday evening 'a large number of tradesmen and principal residents had also turned out to form a torch-light procession to the station to meet the special train bringing the Earl and Lady Stanhope to the town', this inaugurating the railway as a progressive force locally. The Earl was principal landowner locally and was said to have been 'particularly liberal in relation to the land, much of which was given for the purpose'. Work had begun on the line in 1875, the contractor being Mr R T Relf.

The first train to arrive on 'the day of all days', was at 10.00am bringing large numbers of people to the town. It was at midday when the official train arrived, bringing the distinguished guests for the celebration. Whilst an official luncheon was held in a marquee lit by nine gilt and glass chandeliers, with music provided by the Royal Marines Band, 800 members of the Poor were treated to what was described as a 'feast'. Like all communities anxious to benefit from the railway, Holsworthy looked forward to prosperity. The benefits for agriculture were greatly appreciated but there were calls for the extension of the line to the coast at Bude.

On leaving the main Okehampton-Plymouth line at Meldon Junction the Holsworthy line curved away sharply to the north on a radius of 15 chains. The line was carried on a substantial embankment crossing over what later became the A30 trunk road. Thereafter trains entered an equally impressive cutting, once again, curving on 15 chains, this time westward, then to the north west over another embankment to the site of Maddaford Moor Halt eventually opened on 27 July 1926.

JANUARY 20TH, 1879.

Holsworthy Railway Opening.

The following arrangements have been made to Celebrate the Opening Day.

TRADERS' AND GENERAL

PROCESSION

To Parade, headed by Two

MILITARY BANDS.

LUNCHEON

In Edgington's Marquee at 1 p.m.

THE BAND OF THE

ROYAL MARINE LIGHT INFANTRY

Will be in attendance, and will Play during Luncheon, and in the Market Square at intervals. Tickets for Luncheon, 5s. each, obtainablefrom the Secretaries.

GRAND

EVENING CONCERT

In the Marquee at 6.30 p.m. Instrumentalists:

THE

Members of the Royal Marine Band

Pianist:

MR. H. EDWARDS.

Vocalists:

MISS ROBERTSON AND MR. H. GUY.

Tickets, 4s., 2s. 6d., and 1s., obtainable at Jolliffe's, Holsworthy.

A BALL

Will be held in the same Marquee, commencing at 10 p.m. Admission by Tickets, also obtainable at Jolliffe's. Gentlemen, 7s. Ladies, 5s., which includes refreshments. Musicians: Members of the Royal Marine Band.

The Town will be

DECORATED & ILLUMINATED

At considerable expense.

Running north westward across the embankment at Venn Down the line reached Ashbury six miles from Meldon Junction. Here, the main buildings were on the 'down' side; Ashbury was also the main crossing point between Meldon and Halwill, and the only crossing point from 1921 when the Maddaford loop was closed. The goods shed and yard were also on the 'down' side behind the station buildings; the signal box was on the 'up' platform at the Halwill end of the station.

For the majority of the journey on to Halwill, a distance of just under four miles, the line falls on gradients of 1 to 80 and 1 in 78. Over the last half-mile or so into Halwill there is a short climb mostly at 1 in 78.

'Halwill and Beaworthy', 'Halwill Junction', or 'Halwill for Beaworthy', as the station was variously named, might be forgiven for having an identity crisis! It began life as the first named here, became the Junction with the opening of the North Cornwall line in July 1886 and assumed its final name from 1923.

The original station was a very modest structure consisting of two platforms, the main building being on the 'down' side. With the arrival of the North Cornwall line the platforms were said to have been doubled in length and the station generally much enlarged. A bay platform was provided for North Cornwall services and a substantial goods yard was created on the 'up' side to cope with the heavy agricultural/livestock traffic generated by the surrounding area.

At just over three miles distant, the line fell to Dunsland Cross, thirteen miles from Meldon Junction. The main buildings here were also on the 'down' side and were similar in appearance, in what has been called the 'bungalow' style to Ashbury and Halwill. A two mile climb mostly at 1 in 78 and a sharp westerly curve, followed by still further curves, south west, thence north west, at Hollocombe saw the line then dip at 1 in 78 to cross the splendid Holsworthy East Viaduct, a masonry structure of eight arches, standing at a height of 84 feet and 463 feet in length.

The original Holsworthy terminus had its main buildings on the 'up' side, but the arrangement allowed for further extension of the line onward to Bude, as and when, being much in the style, for example, of Helston in West Cornwall where it was hoped to extend southward to the Lizard. Train services in 1879 offered three departures with connections at Okehampton for Waterloo, 7.45am and 12.00 and 2.30pm and one service for Exeter at 6.00pm. First and Second Class passengers on the 7.45pm arrived Waterloo at 2.27pm. Third Class off the 7.45am arrived Waterloo at 4.42pm. Arrivals at Holsworthy were at 10.10, 11.45am, and 3.55pm and 9.00pm, the last two offering service from Waterloo.

Standard Class 4 2-6-4T No. 80059 near Maddaford Moor Halt with the 3.35pm Okehampton-Bude on 4 August, 1964.   *P. Gray*

Activity at Ashbury as Standard Class 4 2-6-4T cross, looking westward towards Halwill, No. 80037 runs in, exchanging the token, with the 3.00pm Padstow-Exeter. The waiting 'down' train was the 5.00pm Okehampton-Bude. 4 August, 1964.
P. Gray

Standard Class 3 2-6-2T No. 82024 leaves Holsworthy with a four coach train for Halwill. The station can just be seen on the far left beyond the viaduct.

M. Esau

With the opening of the railway at Holsworthy, passengers could change to the daily coach service between the town and Bude on the coast. Leaving Bude at 10.30am, the coach connected with the railway to give an arrival at Waterloo of 7.20pm. In the opposite direction, the 9.00am train from Waterloo was met by the 4.00pm coach at Holsworthy giving an arrival at Bude at 5.10pm. The coach service was increased in line with the improved access and availability of Bude, but coach services were no substitute for the railway.

The people of Bude and Stratton thought their hopes were to be fulfilled from 20 August 1883. On that day Parliament passed the Holsworthy and Bude Railway Bill. This line was planned to serve Bridgerule and Stratton, the first sod being ceremonially cut on 31 January 1890. Thereafter, the scheme dissolved and was formally abandoned in May 1892.

Success eventually followed on 6 July 1895 with the LSWR Act to extend into Bude. This line was to follow a different route from that of the earlier, unsuccessful scheme. Running at first west/southwest the railway was to serve the communities of Whitstone to the south of the line and Bridgerule to the north; their station, Whitstone and Bridgerule, mid-way between both places, was some distance from each of them. The main buildings were on the 'down' side and were similar in style to stations on the North Cornwall line. Whitstone and Bridgerule had a goods shed and yard on the 'down' side behind the main buildings; the station, however, was not completed for the opening of the line and only came into service from 1 November 1898, almost three months after Bude itself.

To reach Whitstone and Bridgerule the new line required substantial engineering works in the form of Derriton Viaduct taking the line westward out of Holsworthy. Constructed of pre-cast concrete, 450 feet

in length, it crossed the River Dee on nine arches each of 50 feet span with a height of 95 feet. West of Whitstone and Bridgerule was another viaduct of pre-cast concrete, namely Woolston Viaduct. This was made up of five arches, 250 feet in length, and with a height of 65 feet. Gradients from Holsworthy involved an overall descent mostly at 1 in 82 to Whitstone and Bridgerule, thereafter, a sharper fall at 1 in 73 over some 3 1/2 miles with the line eventually heading in a north westerly direction after Woolston Viaduct to lower lying land across the marshes on the approach to the town and into Bude itself. The line required some heavy cuttings in reaching Whitstone with a further example immediately west of Whitstone and Bridgerule station reaching a depth of 45 feet. For much of the final section northward from Hele Bridge the line needed to be elevated to prevent incidence of flooding.

Bude station was built to generous proportions in the expectation of valuable income from the tourist trade. The result was a stylish red brick structure with Portland stone dressings and quoins accommodating all the requisite offices, first and second class waiting rooms and a refreshment room. A large awning protected the platform before the station building itself whilst the platform, overall, was 570 feet in length; there was also a bay. Outside was a wide approach road and an extensive station yard. This all contributed to the image and substance of a rising resort, confident in its future.

At the approach to the station on the 'down' west side of the line was the locomotive shed with its small coaling stage, watering facilities and turntable, large enough to accommodate the later and very familiar 2-6-0 Class N locomotives introduced from 1924. The goods shed was immediately opposite the water tank and coal stage, level with the far end of the platform on the 'up' side of the line.

74

The Bude Extension opened on 10 August 1898, to the familiar celebrations on the part of a community anxious to participate in railway communication. A Board of Trade inspection carried out by Colonel Mandarin the previous day was complimentary but noted that there was still a certain degree of finishing to be completed. The line had taken some eighteen months to complete. Extremely wet weather had delayed progress in the early stages, but the use of steam navvies assisted construction considerably. The contractor was Messrs John Aird and Co.

From the opening ceremony a special train from Exeter brought dignitaries from the LSWR to the town. Leaving Queen Street at 10.25 the train, composed of the Directors' saloon, two first class coaches and a brake van, arrived at Bude at 12.30pm. An address to the LSWR Directors was presented on behalf of the community recognising the vital role of the railway for the future. Offering their thanks to the company for placing Bude 'in direct communication with busy centres of population and commerce,' the address continued:

We confidently predict that with your assistance Bude will soon take a high position among England's watering places and, we venture to assure you, you may rely on our hearty cooperation in all that will promote the interests of the district.

An alliance of interest between railway and resort was promised and soon after, in 1901, Bude assumed Urban District status and introduced improved standards of public health – water sewerage and drainage projects to enhance the image of the resort.

Initial train services over the new line comprised seven workings in each direction. Arrivals at Bude were as follows: 9.45am, 11.40am, 1.28pm, 3.55pm, 5.19pm, 7.23pm, and 9.50pm. All but the first two arrivals offered connecting services with Waterloo. Departures were at 8.05am, 10.25am, 1.57pm, 3.05pm, 5.45pm, 6.58pm, and 8.45pm. The first four of these trains gave express services to Waterloo.

HOLIDAY SEASON TICKETS

Holiday Season Tickets are now issued solely for holiday purposes to visitors holding ordinary tickets or tourist tickets to **BUDE, LAUNCESTON, WADEBRIDGE or PADSTOW** from any station not less than 50 miles distant, available for one week or longer, and can be obtained on presentation of the backward halves of their ordinary or tourist tickets at Waterloo Station Booking Office and principal London ticket agencies, or at the booking office at the stations named. Holders of tickets available for break of journey at these stations can also obtain the Holiday Season Ticket.

This Holiday Season Ticket is available for any number of journeys between the following stations:— Bude, Whitstone and Bridgerule, Holsworthy, Dunsland Cross, Halwill Junction, Ashwater, Tower Hill, Launceston, Egloskerry, Tresmeer, Camelford, Delabole, Port Isaac Road, St. Kew Highway, Wadebridge, Bodmin, Padstow, and intermediate Halts at the undermentioned fares:—

	3rd Class.
One week	**8s. 9d.**
Two weeks	**14s. 6d.**
Four weeks	**19s. 9d.**

> **HOW TO ENJOY YOUR HOLIDAY ALL THE TIME.**
>
> **MOST PLEASURE AT LEAST COST.**
>
> **TRAVEL WHEN, WHERE AND AS OFTEN AS YOU PLEASE.**

The Cheapest Holiday Travel

CHEAP TICKETS (See Note)(*)

To North Cornwall from London (Waterloo), &c.

TO	Tourist. (Summer only.) 1st	2nd	3rd	Week-End.* 1st	2nd	3rd	Excursion.* Every week during the Summer, also Bank Holidays.
Bude	66/6	41/6	35/9	50/9	31/9	25/6	22/-
Launceston	63/-	40/2	33/9	48/9	30/9	24/6	22/-
Egloskerry							22/-
Tresmeer							22/-
Otterham	66/6	41/6	35/9	51/9	32/6	26/-	22/6
Camelford	67/10	42/6	35/9	52/9	33/-	26/6	23/-
Boscastle	69/2	43/4	36/9				25/6
Tintagel	72/2	46/4	39/9				25/6
Delabole	70/-	43/9	37/6				23/3
Port Isaac Road	71/-	44/6	38/-	54/-	34/-	27/3	24/6
St. Kew Highway							24/6
Wadebridge	72/-	45/8	39/-	56/-	34/9	28/-	25/-
Padstow	73/-	46/8	40/-	56/9	35/9	28/6	25/-
St. Columb } By Coach from	75/-	48/8	42/-				26/-
Newquay } Wadeb'dge	75/-	50/-	42/-				26/-

* Withdrawn during period of War, or until further notice.

Circular Tour 'Rail & Coach' Tickets

40 Tours from London (Waterloo) during the summer months, covering the principal places of interest in Devon and North Cornwall, are also issued.

For full particulars see other announcements.

SPECIMEN TOURS.

TOUR No. 22.

Waterloo to Bude (by Rail throughout); Bude to Boscastle and Camelford (Coach); Camelford to Wadebridge (Rail); Wadebridge to St. Columb (Coach); St. Columb to Wadebridge (Coach); Wadebridge to Camelford (Rail); Camelford to Boscastle and Bude (Coach); Bude to Waterloo (Rail).
1st, 86/-. 2nd, 58/-. 3rd, 51/3.

TOUR No. 6.

Waterloo to Lynton and Lynmouth (by Rail throughout, via Barnstaple); Lynton to Ilfracombe (by "Copps" Coach); Ilfracombe to Bideford (Rail); Bideford to Clovelly, Bude, Boscastle, and Camelford (Coach); Camelford to Wadebridge (Rail); Wadebridge to Newquay (Coach); Newquay to Wadebridge (Coach); Wadebridge to Waterloo (Rail).
1st, 100/2. 2nd, 71/3. 3rd, 63/6.

TOUR No. 37.

Waterloo to Bideford (Rail); Bideford to Clovelly, Bude, Boscastle, and Camelford (Coach); Camelford to Wadebridge (Rail); Wadebridge to Newquay (Coach); Newquay to Wadebridge (Coach); Wadebridge to Camelford (Rail); Camelford to Boscastle, Bude, Clovelly, and Bideford (Coach); Bideford to Waterloo (Rail).
1st, 94/6. 2nd, 67/6. 3rd, 61/9.

An early Southern Railway view of Bude on a summer's afternoon showing the stylish terminal facilities including a refreshment room and first and second class waiting rooms. This all reflected Bude's status as a prestigious holiday resort with its Atlantic Coast imagery.
Cornwall Local Studies Library

By the Summer of 1914 Bude handled ten arrivals and nine departures, and were as follows:

ARRIVALS

9.20am	dep	Halwill	8.45am	
9.20am	dep	Okehampton	8.14am	July-September
11.19am	dep	Exeter Queen St	8.40am	
1.26pm	dep	Halwill	12.50pm	From July 20
2.29pm	dep	Halwill	1.50pm	18 July-29 Sept
3.18pm	dep	Halwill	2.43pm	Tues, Weds, Sats only Until July 11. Weekdays Fri excepted 13 July-30 Sept
4.08pm	dep	Waterloo	11.00am	*North Cornwall/Bude Express* 18 July-29 Sept
5.05pm	dep	Exeter	2.36pm	
7.26pm	dep	Waterloo	1.00pm	
8.33pm	dep	Halwill	7.57pm	July & August
9.52pm	dep	Exeter	7.20pm	

DEPARTURES

7.55am	arr	Waterloo	1.47pm	
9.26am	arr	Waterloo	3.17pm	
11.52am	arr	Halwill	12.43pm	
12.45pm	arr	Halwill	1.25pm	18 July-29 Sept
1.48pm	arr	Waterloo	8.07pm	
3.27pm	arr	Waterloo	10.34pm	
5.50pm	arr	Halwill	6.29pm	
6.45pm	arr	Exeter Queen St	9.27pm	
8.10pm	arr	Halwill	8.50pm	July & August only

In the summer of 1932, the timetable was:

ARRIVALS

8.50am	dep	Halwill	8.15am	
11.17am	dep	Halwill	10.39am	
12.35pm	dep	Halwill	12.00	Not Sats 18 July-9 Sept.
1.02pm	dep	Halwill	12.25pm	From 1 Sept
2.06pm	dep	Halwill	1.32pm	Not Sats. 23 July-10 Sept.
2.24pm	dep	Okehampton	1.14pm	Sats only 23 July-10 Sept.
3.56pm	dep	Waterloo	10.35am	Not Sats 18 July-9 Sept.
4.10pm	dep	Waterloo	11.00am	Sats only 23 July-10 Sept.
4.56pm	dep	Waterloo	11.00am	
6.10pm	dep	Exeter	3.52pm	Fri only 22 July-9 Sept
7.03pm	dep	Okehampton	5.52pm	Not Sats. 23 July-10 Sept.
7.28pm	dep	Okehampton	6.27pm	Sats only 23 July-10 Sept.
8.56pm	dep	Okehampton	7.45pm	
9.50pm	dep	Holsworthy	9.32pm	Thur/Sat. only 21 July-10 Sept.

DEPARTURES

7.20am	arr	Okehampton	8.38am	
9.40am	arr	Okehampton	11.09am	(Exeter, Mon-Fri, 18 July - 9 Sept.
10.38am	arr	Waterloo	4.13pm	Not Sats 18 July-9 Sept.
10.40am	arr	Waterloo	4.20pm	Sats only 23 July-9 Sept.
11.18am	arr	Waterloo	5.09pm	Fri only 22 July-9 Sept
12.40pm	arr	Halwill	1.19pm	Not Sats 23 July-10 Sept.
1.40pm	arr	Okehampton	2.47pm	Not Sats 23 July-10 Sept.
1.44pm	arr	Halwill	2.25pm	Not Sats 23 July-10 Sept.
3.10pm	arr	Halwill	3.52pm	Sats only 23 July-10 Sept.
3.15pm	arr	Halwill	4.01pm	Not Sats 23 July-10 Sept.
5.30pm	arr	Halwill	6.10pm	Not Sats 18 July-9 Sept.
5.48pm	arr	Halwill	6.27pm	Sat only 23 July-10 Sept.
7.00pm	arr	Halwill	7.41pm	
9.05pm	arr	Holsworthy	9.26pm	Thurs/Sats 21 July-10 Sept.

The weekday/Saturday timetable for 1932 did not include the impressive list below of Summer Sunday excursions available from and to Bude. These were many and varied reflecting well on both railway and resort:

BUDE DEPARTURES

10.00am Half-day excursion to Bournemouth on 24 July, 21 August and 18 September. (Return dep. 7.45pm).

10.00am Half-day excursion to Plymouth on 31 July, 28 August and 25 September. (Return dep. 8.05pm).

10.00am Half-day excursion to Ilfracombe (via Torrington) on 7 August and 4 September. (Return 7.30pm).

10.00am Half-day excursion to Exeter and Paignton on 17 July and 11 September. (Return dep. 7.10pm).

10.00am Half-day excursion to Bristol on 14 August. (Return, dep. Bristol, 7.45pm).

BUDE ARRIVALS

12.21pm Half-day excursion from Plymouth on 24 July, 21 August and 18 September. (Return dep. 8.10pm).

1.18pm Half-day excursion from Exmouth on 17 July, 14 August and 11 September. (Return dep. 8.25pm).

1.28pm Half-day excursion from Ilfracombe on 3 July, 28 August and 25 September. (Return dep. 7.35pm).

2.08pm Half-day excursion from Salisbury on 7 August and 4 September. (Return dep. Bude 7.35pm).

Standard Class 3 2-6-2T No. 82018 climbs away from Bude with a train for Halwill late in the life of the line.   *M. Esau*

Some forty years after 1914, through both the Grouping under the Southern Railway and Nationalisation as British Railways Southern Region, the timetable showed a definite continuity of structure. The Summer Saturday service for 1955 offered the following:

ARRIVALS

6.49am	dep Waterloo	12.35am	16 July-10 Sept
7.49am	dep Halwill	7.15am	
9.25am	dep Halwill	8.53am	
11.33am	dep Okehampton	10.15am	
1.23pm	dep Waterloo	7.33am	2 July-27 Aug
2.23pm	dep Okehampton	1.18pm	
3.54pm	dep Waterloo	10.35am	*Atlantic Coast Express*
5.09pm	dep Waterloo	11.15am	
7.00pm	dep Okehampton	5.51pm	
8.55pm	dep Okehampton	7.45pm	

DEPARTURES

7.58am	arr Okehampton	9.20am	
9.00am	arr Waterloo	3.04pm	
9.30am	arr Waterloo	3.23pm	
11.45am	arr Waterloo	5.09pm	*ACE* 16 July-10 Sept
11.45am	arr Waterloo	5.24pm	Until 9 July & 17 Sept
2.00pm	arr Waterloo	8.25pm	
3.13pm	arr Okehampton	4.37pm	
5.32pm	arr Halwill	6.11pm	
7.02pm	arr Okehampton	8.29pm	

This year, 1955, represents the post-war peak performance period for services to and from Bude. As with all railway routes in the West Country the following decade brought sweeping changes. The shifts in regional control have been referred to elsewhere, and, as with the North Cornwall line, steam traction ceased in January 1965. Later that same year, Bude saw the last of its through trains when the Summer Saturday only Paddington to Bude and Ilfracombe, a feature of the 1965 timetable, was withdrawn. The *Atlantic Coast Express*, of course, had made its last run on 5 September 1964. The very end for the railway at Bude came in 1966. Saturday 1 October that year saw the departure of the last train. It joined the final working from Wadebridge over the North Cornwall line at Halwill, and the junction which had, up to a year or so before, handled trains for Wadebridge and Padstow, Bude and Torrington (from July 1925), the hub of services for the entire system in North Cornwall, passed into history.

Whitstone and Bridgerule on 2 January, 1965, the penultimate day of steam operation on the Southern lines west of Exeter. The locomotive was No. 82040; the train was the 2.42pm Halwill-Bude.   *P. Gray*

More activity on the last day but one for steam. Standard Class 4 No. 75025 runs round its train at Bude – the 12.10pm from Okehampton. 2 January, 1965.   *P. Gray*

PHOTOGRAPHING
CARVED STONES

A Practical Guide to
Recording Scotland's Past

TOM E GRAY AND LESLEY M FERGUSON

The National Committee
on the Carved Stones of Scotland

in association with

HISTORIC SCOTLAND

The Pinkfoot Press
Balgavies, Angus
1997

First published in Scotland in 1997 by
The Pinkfoot Press
Balgavies, Forfar, Angus DD8 2TH

© National Committee on the Carved Stones
of Scotland and individual contributors, 1997

ISBN 1 874012 14 8

Typesetting and origination: The Pinkfoot Press
Printed by Burns Harris and Findlay Ltd, Dundee

CONTENTS

ILLUSTRATIONS

THE PROTECTION OF CARVED STONES

The unparalleled geological treasury which made Scotland the home of modern scientific geology also gave it the potential for an unmatched heritage of carved stone monuments and architectural ornament. An abundance of carving and sculpture provides a record literally 'set in stone' of successive waves of cultural enrichment, a uniquely valuable insight into Northern European artistic development. The prehistoric and carved stone monuments of the Pictish and early Christian periods are well known, but Scotland boasts equally important collections of medieval and post-medieval carved stones.

Sadly this rich heritage has not always been recognised or preserved as it deserves. Even today, when a large number of carved stones are statutorily protected, either by scheduling or listing, many are neglected and in poor condition.

Even where carved stones appear to be in good condition, they may be adversely affected by well-intentioned attempts at conservation. They may be irreparably damaged by lifting, or moving fallen stones to set them upright, excavating around them to expose hidden parts or attempting to clean off moss and lichen to enable a better view. All such 'contact' operations should only be carried out by qualified and experienced conservators and may, indeed, require formal permission in the form of Scheduled Monument or Listed Building Consent.

Historic stone surfaces may be surprisingly friable or tend to delaminate. The roots of mosses and lichens in particular can be deeply embedded into the stones, and removal by brushing or scraping can blur important historic detail, or efface it permanently. Similarly, the abrasion required by the application of chalk, making

presses, moulds or rubbings can lead to grain loss. Irreversible damage and discoloration can also be caused by waxes and dyes, even when carried out with the best of intentions by those who want to appreciate the beauty of the stones. Spraying with chemicals, or just wetting with water, can also introduce harmful salts into delicate stones, and make them susceptible to frost and crystallisation damage, and accelerate decay.

As part of its ongoing nationwide programme of conservation research and education, Historic Scotland is keen to encourage the recording of carved stones, but this needs to be undertaken with care and appropriate guidance. Photographic records, by professional and amateur alike, provide a crucially important resource in protecting and preserving carved stones. It is precisely because it does not require physical contact or intervention that photography is such a valuable primary tool for recording the condition of historic carved stones.

Supported by Historic Scotland, this publication by the National Committee on the Carved Stones of Scotland is to be welcomed by all who care for Scotland's heritage. Written by the well-known photographer of carved stones, Tom E Gray, and by Lesley M Ferguson of the Royal Commission on the Ancient and Historical Monuments of Scotland, it is illustrated by Tom E Gray, Ian Gray, formerly of Historic Scotland, and the Photographic Department of RCAHMS, and edited by Anna Ritchie.

Ingval Maxwell   May 1997

Director, Technical Conservation,
Research and Education Division
Historic Scotland

PHOTOGRAPHIC RECORDING OF CARVED STONES

TOM E GRAY

The background to my advice on photo-recording is forty years in and around professional photography, including twelve years of museum, art gallery, and architectural work. I have also had a life-long interest in prehistory and history prior to about AD 1200. All this was combined in eight years of retiral in a concentrated project to photograph as much Dark Age sculpture as possible. This has been accomplished using relatively simple equipment such as many enthusiastic amateur photographers might possess.

This booklet is aimed at members of local societies or individuals who wish to make a photo record of medieval carved stones of the period from about AD 500 to the 16th century. A vast photographic knowledge is not required, and it is worth bearing in mind that even the simplest snapshot is a valuable record of a sculptured stone in time, place, and condition. For the more advanced work many societies will often have at least one enthusiastic photographer with the right kind of equipment, and if not it may be consoling to know that a suitable medium format camera with a couple of flashes can be had second-hand for less than the price of a good 35 mm single-lens reflex.

Much of what is written here will apply to the recording of later material, but this is covered very competently in Willsher (1985).

Photography is a non-destructive method of creating a permanent record, which, if properly done, can result in a print showing detail on worn stones that is scarcely visible, if at all, to the eye (illus 1) and which can then be used to produce a drawing if so wished.

1 *Fetterangus, NGR (National Grid Reference) NJ 981505, Allen and Anderson 1903, 164. A stone which the literature suggests is illegible but grazing light from one flash has revealed all three elements, cauldron, mirror case and harp-like object. This was done at dusk when the light was so poor that I had to use a powerful torch on the stone to set up the shot in the camera viewfinder. Such work could be done with the 35mm camera with its flash synchronisation limited to 1/60th second. TE Gray, neg no 3711, Sept 1990.*

CAMERAS

The very widely used 35 mm single-lens reflexes such as Pentax, Olympus, Canon, and Nikon are excellent for much of this work when using natural light alone. The auto-compacts by the same makers, depending on make, price and specification, are also useful, although their usefulness may be limited to very dull days or night-time. The reason for this will be explained in greater detail in the practical section on lighting. This certainly limits the ability to carry out a sustained project on a lot of stones in a variety of working situations, where the object is to produce a quantity of top-quality monochrome work for archive or reproduction. The built-in flashes on many cameras are of little or no use in this field.

The technique of multiple separate flashes combined with daylight, used at an oblique angle to reveal the detail on very worn stones, is best used with a camera with between-lens shutter which synchronises up to 1/500 sec. This almost limits you to 120 rollfilm cameras of Mamiyaflex, Rolleiflex, Bronica, Hasselblad type, but it is certainly the method which yields the most satisfying rendering of detail on worn stones which is sometimes almost invisible to the eye. Such rollfilm equipment need not be expensive. Rolleiflex/Yashicamat/Minolta Autocord/Mamiyaflex twin lens models can be had second-hand in good condition for less than the cost of many modern 35 mm single-lens reflexes, and a couple of suitable flashguns need not cost the earth. Many local history groups or societies are likely to have at least one enthusiastic amateur photographer member who possesses such equipment. Specialist photographic equipment shops are the most reliable source of information and help, and they often have such equipment for sale second-hand.

Special terms used in this booklet are explained in the glossary.

2 Collessie, NGR NO 293133. A stone 2.7 m (9 ft) high where even a 2 m tripod was barely tall enough. I would have liked to get up level with the top of the stone to reveal more clearly in a detail shot the unusual hair style. A single flash. TE Gray, neg no 3720/1, Nov 1990.

TRIPODS

The use of a good solid tripod is essential for careful, accurate, considered work. One which extends to a height of seven feet or more can be very useful for sculpture in an elevated position (illus 2), but by implication you also need a light-weight set of aluminium steps in order to be able to see in the camera viewfinder!

LENSES

Probably 75 per cent of photographs of carved stones can be taken with the standard lens, ie 50 mm on 35 mm, 80 mm on 120 rollfilm.

For stones in a confined space or behind railings, a wide-angle lens can save the day. Moderately wide-angle lenses (24 or 28 mm on

35mm film, 50mm on 120 rollfilm) are virtually distortion free. Some of these lenses are available with a perspective control movement, which enables correction to be made on the negative to avoid the convergence of architectural verticals. Those who do not possess perspective control lenses but who do their own darkroom work will find that correction under the enlarger of distorted verticals works well. The writer has done this for many years using a home-made calibrated tilting baseboard with complete satisfaction.

Extreme wide-angle lenses can produce distortion problems.

Very occasionally for stones in an awkward position, high on a wall, or in difficult landscape, a longer focal length can be used.

FLASHES AND SUPPORTS

Flashguns powerful enough to have a guide number of at least 110, or preferably 150, in feet are necessary for the flash technique described later, when the use of the guide number will be explained. Lighting stands to support these guns are necessary, as are long leads (at least 4m). Unfortunately modern photo lighting stands are U-section alloy. The writer uses two ancient (pre-Second World War!) steel stands, and steel music stands have been seen which could be suitably robust and might be adapted for photography. Lightweight camera tripods with individually adjustable legs could prove very satisfactory for supporting the flashes.

It should be evident by now that to carry camera, meter, tripod, and two flashes with stands, any distance, a helper could be very desirable! The writer has not yet found an entirely suitable method of carrying all this equipment, sometimes walking ten-mile round trips to remote preaching crosses! It is the awkward shapes of tripod and lighting stands rather than the overall weight that causes problems. A rucksack can be used for camera, flash gear, and ancillary bits and pieces, but tripod and lighting stands are less easy to accommodate. Golf and shopping trolleys have been tried but are pretty useless on rough terrain.

For work indoors, where power points are available, a couple of modern domestic light stands fitted with 100-watt reflector-backed floods are ideal and allow the operator to study exactly what the light is doing in the way of revealing detail. Exposures may be several seconds but this is no problem with a firmly supported camera. If the budget extends to it, proper photo lighting stands using photoflood lamps permit shorter exposures but really offer little other advantage.

MATERIALS

The professional archaeology/art history requirement for an archive is still heavily in favour of monochrome photography, for its flexibility and long-term stability, and for the crisp contrast which renders the stones so well. Film of speed 100 ASA is ideal, especially if the camera is on a tripod. If the camera has to be hand held, or if the light is very dull, modern fast monochrome films of 400 ASA are sufficiently grain-free to be employed with every confidence, especially as it is unlikely that prints larger than 13 x 18cm (5 x 7ins) or 20 x 25cm (8 x 10ins) will be required.

For those who process their own monochrome film, there is little point in chopping and changing developers and techniques. Indeed everything is to be gained by standardising on one film, and a developer of D76 type, and getting to know the combination thoroughly.

Most amateur cameras nowadays are loaded with colour negative film, and the laboratory printing of these is of quite high and consistent quality, sufficient for recording. There is still a slight question, however, about the long-term stability and sharpness of the negatives and prints, as compared to monochrome.

For those readers who do their own black and white printing, it is well worth noting that, as stones are almost monochrome anyway (grey stone, green grass), these colour negatives print perfectly well as black-and-white on monochrome variable contrast paper, Kodak Polymax or the equivalent.

Colour transparency film can be highly desirable for lecturing purposes. Again the question of long-term stability of the results arises. Kodachrome film is still considered to be best in this field; a life of 100 years has been quoted, with other makes of film close on its heels (eg Agfa, Fuji). Choice of film speed to be used with either negative or transparency colour film is much the same as with monochrome, somewhere around 64–100 ASA being first choice for quality and sharpness, and the faster ones in reserve for awkward situations.

To cover all eventualities, two cameras, or one of the rollfilm cameras which allows the use of interchangeable film backs, will allow both monochrome and colour to be tackled.

3 *Aberlemno no 3, NGR NO 552558, Allen and Anderson 1903, 214. Using sunlight only. Had I used a standard lens, I would have had to risk life and limb in the middle of the road! This was one of those few occasions in this work where a telephoto lens was useful, allowing me to stand on the opposite verge. TE Gray, neg no 4015/2, Aug 1993.*

LIGHTING

Of all the factors involved in the production of first-class results showing good tonal rendering, and most important of all, fine detail, especially in worn stones and sculpture, the right lighting comes highest in the list. The ideal lighting is almost invariably a crisp clear sunlight at a grazing angle of 5 to 15 degrees across the surface of the stone (illus 3). Stones with high relief usually demand less of a grazing angle in order that detail is not lost in the deeper hollows. The worn incised Pictish symbol stones and simple early Christian crosses need a very sharp grazing angle indeed to bring out features which can scarcely be seen by eye.

To be sure of the correct lighting usually means a prior visit to the stone, compass in hand, to measure the orientation of the main face. Referring to the Sun Direction Indicator diagram (illus 4), it is then possible to forecast to within about 20 minutes just when one should be on the spot for the best sharp-angled light. Arrive a little early and watch the best lighting angle gradually develop.

All of what has been said so far about lighting obviously applies to those stones which are suitably placed to get the correct angle of sunlight at some time of the day. Working in sunlight, especially when there are white clouds around, fulfils one of the prime requirements of fine photography. This is that the amount of light falling on the subject from the sun should be three or four times stronger than that light which reaches the shadows, reflected from the white clouds. This is what skilled photographers call the ideal 4–1 lighting contrast. In these natural light situations the modern 35mm single-lens reflex will do a first-class job.

But what of those stones which face north, or are in a dark wood (illus 5) or are inside? Or you need to do six stones in one day and you cannot be at all of them at the right time for the sun?

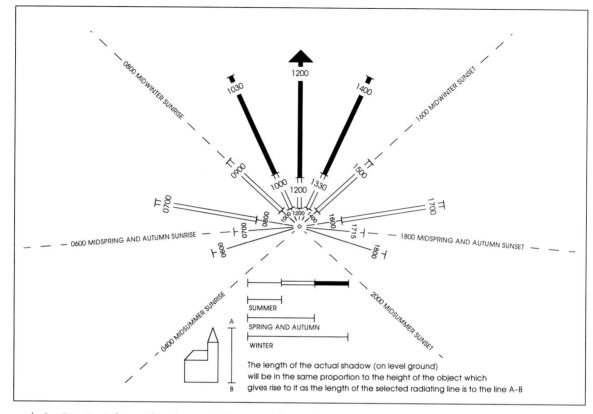

4 Sun Direction Indicator. This, when used with a compass bearing from the major face of a stone, allows the photographer to work out to within about 20 minutes when to arrive to get the angle of the sun which gives best rendering of detail.

Or the stone may have carving on front, back and sides, which could mean four visits if you want to get the correct angle of sunlight for all four, which may never happen!

If you are working with the camera on a tripod in poor light, it is perfectly possible to use a longer exposure, and you will get a record of the stone, but, as the lighting is not the most suitable, the end result will indeed show that the stone exists, but it will almost certainly not bring out the detail of the stone, especially if it is badly worn.

FLASH COMBINED WITH DAYLIGHT, THE PERFECT ANSWER

It is here that single or multiple flash comes into its own. Flashguns come in two forms. The entirely automatic gun incorporates a small photocell in the body of the gun, which 'reads' the light reflected back from the subject and shuts off the flash when the correct exposure is reached.

This is almost entirely unsuited to our work in that, first, they are not usually sufficiently powerful in light output, and secondly, due to the specialist nature of this photography and the acute angle at which the lights are used, the auto exposure is usually wrong.

The second type of gun is one which has an automatic function but can also be set to manual operation. At that setting, it gives its highest power at a fixed level and also allows the photographer to choose his own camera settings. This type is an essential choice for the serious worker. Two flashguns of the Metz 45 type and power, mounted on telescopic stands, remote from the camera, and fired by means of long leads or slave units from the camera, give the greatest flexibility and the finest results. The photographer is independent of sunlight, and the best lighting angle can always be achieved.

As these units are used at such an acute angle, normal methods of working out the aperture to

5 *Glamis no 1, NGR NO 395465, Allen and Anderson 1903, 221. An example of a stone in a dark wood with two sides to be photographed, near impossible to do well without flash. TE Gray, neg no 3558/2, Nov 1989.*

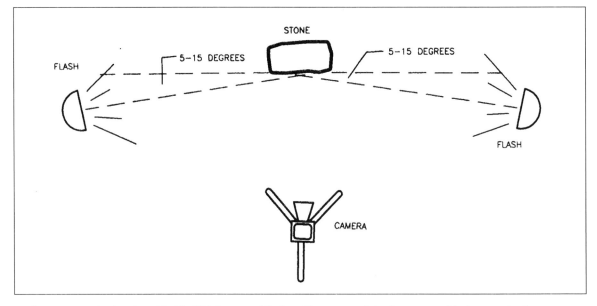

6 *Diagrammatic plan view of the ideal lighting set-up. Whether with one or two lights the aperture of the lens remains the same. The addition of barn doors on the flashes will prevent light reaching the camera lens and causing flare.*

use, using the flash guide number, are only a very rough guide. Flash units are given a guide number for a particular film speed by the maker, and one divides the guide number by the distance in feet or metres from flash to subject to arrive at the correct aperture to use on the camera. For example, the instructions for my own Metz 45 guns suggest a guide number of 45 in metres for 100 ASA film. Using it at 1.8m from the subject and dividing the guide number 45 by 1.8 results in an aperture on the camera of F/25. This would be the correct setting if the flash were positioned near the camera, whereas, because of the light loss resulting from the acute lighting angle of perhaps 5 degrees, in reality I use F/8.

If you intend to do a lot of such photography, it is very wise to do a trial run in dull light or inside on a stone, using a flash at one or both sides at a measured 1.8m and bracketing the calculated aperture by three stops (illus 6 and 7). Choose the best negative and from then on you know exactly which stop to use. If, because of lack of space perhaps, the flashes have to be at 1.35m, the aperture will be one stop smaller. I find that I work almost invariably with the flashes at either 1.8 or 1.35 metres and thus know exactly which camera settings to use.

7 *Aldbar stone, NGR NO 574580, Allen and Anderson 1903, 245. Now in Brechin Cathedral. A fine example of the use of two flashes. It is well worth studying closely the lighting in every photograph to see if you can decide just how acute was the angle of the light or lights. TE Gray, neg no 4012/1, Aug 1993.*

As a guide to assist in initial trials, it may be useful to know that I use one Metz 45 flash at 1.8m either side, 100 ASA film, and an aperture of F/8. On a trial run, if you use my suggestion of F/8, then a one-stop bracketing, F5.6–F/8–F/11, will be sufficient. If your gun has a maker's guide number that is different from the 45 metres of the Metz 45, or if you use a different film speed, some simple mathematics should result in the correct aperture.

This is not the end however. In order to balance the flash with daylight to fill some detail in the shadows, a meter reading of the daylight is taken, using a separate meter's incident light attachment, or the camera's built-in meter. The shutter speed indicated by the meter for the chosen flash aperture should be noted, and this should then be quartered, ie 1/60 becomes 1/250. This gives the correct lighting contrast of 4–1 as discussed in the section dealing with photography in sunlight.

You will now see why it was suggested in the section on EQUIPMENT that limited flash synchronisation of 35mm reflexes limits the available lighting choice. The meter daylight reading would have to be no faster than 1/15 for a camera whose fastest flash synch speed was 1/60. In other words, you will always need to work in dull light, very early or late in the day, or even in the dark. This brings its own problems, as some kind of light must be provided in order to see the image in the camera viewfinder to frame and focus. A powerful torch will serve. In contrast, the use of a camera with between lens shutter synchronising at all speeds up to 1/500 sec allows working in bright light but with all the advantages of full control of lighting from one or two flashes.

There are occasions, perhaps when one side of a stone is close to a wall, when it is impossible to use two flashes. High quality results can still be achieved with the one flash (at the same aperture as used for both) and using a meter reading to get the correct balance of daylight. A great deal of fine work can be done with only one flash (illus 8), with a second kept in reserve for really difficult subjects.

8 *Rossie, NGR NO 291308, Allen and Anderson 1903, 306. Because of the stone's proximity to a wall, only one flash could be used, which nevertheless revealed all the detail on this fine stone. Shots inside, such as this and Aldbar, come well within the capability of the 35mm camera with its limited flash synchronisation. To visit stones such as this on a private estate, permission should be sought in advance. TE Gray, neg no 3667/1, June 1990.*

In the early stages of carrying out this photography, it can be difficult to decide the correct angle for the lighting. In dull light or indoors a powerful torch can be directed across the face of the stone and moved around until maximum relief and detail is achieved. The flash is then placed in this position.

INSCRIPTIONS

Not only is it necessary to set the flashes to the correct raking angle across the surface of the stone, but it is also necessary to light across the predominant lines, particularly with inscriptions such as oghams. Any lines at right angles to the lighting direction will show up very clearly, but those parallel to the lighting direction may disappear. The strokes of ogham (illus 10) and those of the Latin alphabet are at various angles, and it may be necessary to take several shots with the flashes at slightly different angles, each of which will reveal different detail. The end result might be a drawing combining the detail revealed by each print. Some oghams use the corner of the stone as the base line, and it is sometimes possible to use one flash on the edge of the stone and the second on the face as in the drawing (illus 11). The same technique can be used to create revealing lighting on two sides of a four-sided stone (illus 12). The archaeologist/art

9 *Tote, Skye, used as a door-jamb in Tote until moved in 1880 to the present position, NGR NG 421490. An example of using a single flash on a dull day to simulate sunlight, which reveals every detail, even the much worn comb at bottom right. Taken on a typical Skye day, with a poly bag over the flash and camera, but not covering the lens, to keep out the rain! TE Gray, neg no 3830/1, Oct 1991.*

10 *Golspie, NGR NH 837002, now in Dunrobin Castle, Allen and Anderson 1903, 48. The two-flash lighting has revealed the ogham inscription as well as all the other interesting detail. TE Gray, neg no 3658/4, June 1990.*

historian may need the multiple exposure approach with different lighting angles in order to extract the maximum amount of information.

This description of the use of two flashes may seem very complicated to those with limited photographic experience. The advantages are that it frees you of the necessity of having to depend on sunlight, allows a number of shots to be done in one day, deals easily with those situations where sunlight direction is unsuitable, or where the stone is in a poorly lit situation, and gives easily the finest rendering of worn detail.

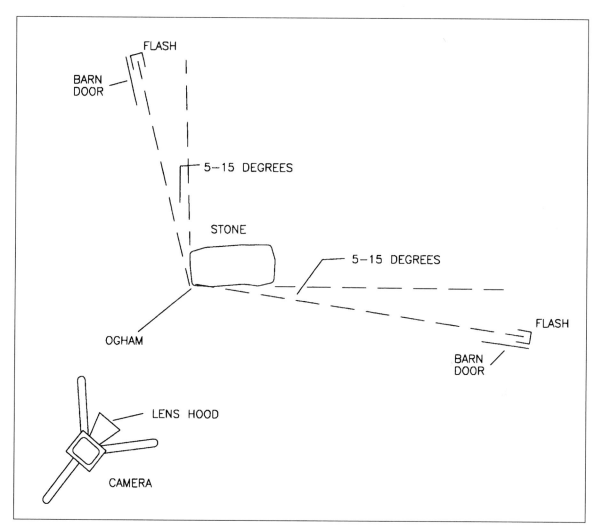

11 *Diagram showing how to light an ogham inscription which extends round the corner of the stone. The same lighting set-up yields very attractive and revealing results with stones which have a wealth of carving on all four sides, for two sides can be included in one shot, see illus 12.*

PICTORIAL PHOTOGRAPHS

Some stones lend themselves to a more artistic or pictorial presentation, and such photos can enliven an article, book or slide talk in which the majority of photos are straight records. One approach is to capture the attractive historical landscape dominated by the stone, for example the Dupplin Cross in its setting (illus 13). Again the use of one flash away from the camera, perhaps laid on the ground shining up at the stone to simulate firelight, can evoke some ancient ceremony (illus 14).

DIMENSIONAL ACCURACY

Drawings of stones, such as those superb examples produced by RCAHMS, are very often based on photographs. For this purpose, and to get the necessary dimensional accuracy, the camera back should be parallel to the principal plane of the stone. I rarely use ranging poles or measures, because the dimensions of the vast majority of early medieval stones are already recorded by Allen and Anderson (1903) and elsewhere. For new finds, it will help the archives if you fill in an information sheet such as that at the end of this booklet.

12   Abercorn no 1, NGR 082792. This shows the fine result obtained by using two flashes set up as in illus 11. TE Gray neg no 3734/1, Feb 1991.

13   Dupplin, NGR NO 051189, Allen and Anderson 1903, 319. The stone in its commanding setting looking over the valley of the Earn. This is the type of shot which needs a small APERTURE to give great DEPTH OF FIELD, see Glossary. TE Gray, neg no 3597/2, March 1990.

14 *The Craw Stane, Rhynie, NGR NJ 496263, Allen and Anderson 1903, 182. This was 'dramatised' by laying a single flash on the ground pointing up to simulate firelight. I like to dramatise a stone when it lends itself to this treatment, provided that there is no sacrifice of the essential detail. Such shots lend excitement and variety to the illustrations in a book or slide lecture. TE Gray, neg no 3722/1, Nov 1990.*

ARCHITECTURAL RECORDING

So far all the recommendations have been aimed specifically at photographing what are by far the most plentiful carved memorials of the period AD 500–1000. These are incised or shallow relief carved stones, often located singly in fields or woods or in graveyards throughout Scotland, whether they be Pictish in the east, Dalriadan in the west, or of British or Anglian influence south of the Central Belt.

From about AD 1000 to 1400, the material crying out for recording is very different in character. We now find ourselves concerned with architecture or architectural fragments, whether in and around ruined or unused churches such as Restenneth, or intact examples such as Dalmeny. Items such as mason's marks or shallow relief carvings can still be treated as described already, but doorways, windows, and other architectural detail are rather more easily photographed. Flashlights are rarely necessary, and crisp clear sunlight renders much of this material in an entirely satisfactory fashion (illus 15).

As churches are usually orientated approximately east-west it is not difficult with a little knowledge of the building and the help of the Sun Direction Indicator to estimate at what time of day sunlight will best reveal the detail. The heavily carved arch of a south doorway such as those at Dalmeny or Kirkliston probably needs two photos to extract maximum detail, for mid-morning sun will reveal detail in the western half of the arch,

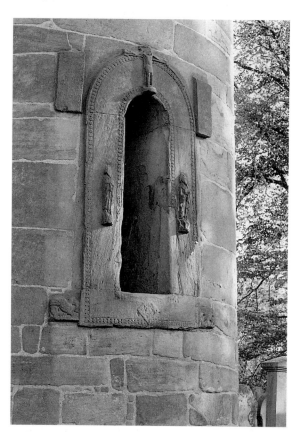

15 *Door of the round tower at Brechin Cathedral.*
A simple shot using sunlight to point up the essential detail.
TE Gray, neg no 2842, Nov 1977.

Ideally negatives should be accompanied by contact sheets, which should have full details on the back, stone name, location, map reference of find place and current site, date when photographed. Documentary references could also be included, eg Allen and Anderson 1903, p.342. A card or computer-based index is essential.

PERMISSION TO PHOTOGRAPH

When stones are in private hands on estates or in museums, permission should be sought by letter well in advance of the intended visit. Proof of the seriousness of the project, in the form of letters, publications or prints of other stones, should be on hand for production if necessary. Very occasionally, for one reason or another, you may have to arrive on an estate unannounced; again proof of serious intent should be produced, and permission sought in a courteous manner. But this is not an approach to be regularly used or recommended. Afterwards prints should be sent to owners with compliments to cement a good relationship.

and mid-afternoon sun the eastern half (illus 16). With all other exterior features a reasonable knowledge of the building together with the use of the Sun Direction Indicator will enable the photographer to be on site at the right time for best results.

For interior detail, the directional light afforded by windows usually gives a very satisfactory relief to the work to be photographed. Because the photographer is much less dependent on flash lighting, lack of full flash synchronisation on most modern 35 mm single-lens reflexes is not in this case a hindrance to the use of such cameras, and they are capable of producing informative and lasting records. For those doing their own monochrome printing, the use of a tilting baseboard helps considerably to correct converging verticals when necessary, as mentioned in the section on Lenses.

16 (opposite) *Dalmeny church south door. To get all the detail in the arch two photographs are necessary, one mid-morning, and a second mid-afternoon. A study of the lines on the Sun Direction Indicator in relation to the east, south or west walls will enable an estimate of the best time to be made to within about 20 minutes. TE Gray, neg no 504, Aug 1954.*

COPYRIGHT

This is a minefield area but in brief, some years ago copyright law was changed to give freelance photographers the same rights as all other 'artists'. When the photographer presses the shutter release, the end result is his or her copyright, even if commissioned and paid to do a job. More recently the duration of copyright has been extended, to bring Britain into line with other European countries, to 70 years after the death of the photographer. Only one museum in my experience insisted that copyright had to be assigned to them before permission to photograph would be granted, and this was a recent change in their rules. But photographers are likely to be faced with this situation more and more in museums that are under pressure to increase revenue, and in some cases the museum may demand the copyright fee in any publications. In all other situations, copyright remains with the photographer, but again in the case of publication it is common courtesy to acknowledge the source, and the help and co-operation received. Historic Scotland only ask that in publications acknowledgement should be made to them in the case of scheduled monuments.

CHECK LIST OF EQUIPMENT FOR FIELD OUTINGS

BARN DOORS Pieces of thin light-weight black plastic card (can be bought in model shops) which can be attached parallel to the side of the flashguns with Velcro to prevent the flash shining into the lens.

BATTERIES A set of spares for flashguns, and for camera and meter if battery operated, should always be carried.

CABLE SHUTTER RELEASE Ensures shake-free results with exposures on the tripod.

CAMERA Plus standard lens, preferably one with a shutter which synchronises for flash up to 1/500 sec, for complete ease of working in any light with flash.

CLEAR POLY BAGS Used to cover flash gear and camera in rain, such bags make no noticeable difference to the amount of light from the flash. Do not cover the camera lens with the bag, it could spoil sharpness and cause flare. An umbrella is also useful.

COMPASS plus SUN DIRECTION INDICATOR A bearing can be taken on the main face of any sculpture, this bearing compared with the lines on the Sun Direction Indicator and the time chosen on the line which is likely to give the best raking light for showing maximum detail. Can be accurate to within about twenty minutes.

ELECTRONIC FLASHES Preferably those powerful enough to yield a Guide Number of about 45 m (150 feet) with 100 ASA speed films. A single flash will yield highly satisfactory results for the record, but two allow even more ambitious work.

17 Tombstone, Abercorn. Taken on a dull day when I had a number of stones to photograph. Using one flash to simulate sunlight and give some contrast, I was able to do the lot. TE Gray, neg no 3560/1, Nov 1989.

EXTENSION CABLES Connected to camera and flash, they will fire the flash when the shutter is released.

LENS HOOD A necessary item to shield the lens from the flash or flashes which are forward of the camera. It is useful to have a piece of black card of approx 155 x 205 mm (6 x 6 ins) which can also be used as an additional insurance to prevent light from reaching the lens and causing flare. See also BARN DOORS.

LIGHT METER Measures the strength of the daylight in order to adjust the shutter speed to give the correct 4–1 lighting balance with flash. A flash meter is not necessary, as a simple trial run will establish the aperture to be used for one or two flashes at 1.8 m (6 feet) and this remains constant thereafter.

LIGHTING STANDS These should preferably be of steel, especially for hill slopes. The alternative might be light camera tripods, the legs of which can be individually adjusted to deal with uneven ground. Lighting stands can be dispensed with if one has an assistant who can be relied upon to hold the flash steady at the correct distance and angle. Such an assistant can be pressed into service to help carry all the heavy gear!

NOTEBOOK AND PEN Necessary for recording technical details such as distance of flashes from subject, lens aperture, shutter speed, and also for recording stone details such as dimensions if it is a new find, current condition, whether in original position, OS map reference, and of course date of photography.

POWERFUL TORCHES Useful in weaker light to establish the correct angle of light to reveal maximum detail, the flash then being placed in this position. It can also be necessary when the light is rather poor, to put sufficient light on the subject in order to see the image in the camera viewfinder for framing and focusing. Useful too for seeing camera and flash settings in poor light.

SLAVE UNITS One of these, when attached to a second flash, will react to the brilliant burst of light from the first flash, thus firing the second. It is possible to dispense with extension leads by using slave units on the remote flashes fired by a weak flash from the camera.

SOFT CARPET BRUSH For light gentle brushing of loose dirt and debris from the surface of the stone. No more than this should ever be attempted, and if the stone is friable even this should be avoided. Never try to remove lichen, this is a job for experienced conservators.

SPIRIT LEVEL A small one can be had which slips in the camera's shoe, (a fitting on top of cameras for taking a variety of accessories), useful for ensuring that the camera is level.

TAPE MEASURE Ensures that flashes are at the required distance from the subject. Experience suggests that this is almost invariably 1.8 m or 1.35 m (6 ft or 4.5 feet), for which distances a previous trial run has given the correct aperture to use. Also for taking the dimensions of stones where this information is not already recorded in ECMS or elsewhere.

TELEPHOTO LENS Can very occasionally be useful if the sculpture is high up on a wall or in an otherwise inaccessible position.

TOOLS A set of small instrument screwdrivers, some Blu-tack, lens brush, lens cleaning tissue, a small handbag mirror for seeing equipment settings in awkward corners; in other words a handy little kit of bits and pieces for dealing with the odd emergency.

TRIPOD This should preferably be heavy and substantial, extending to about 2 m (7 feet) or beyond. A lighter weight tripod is useful to have for long walks to distant preaching crosses. A lightweight aluminium stepladder may be needed to see into the viewfinder.

WIDE-ANGLE LENS Very useful in restricted situations.

18 *Columba's Cave, Ellary, Argyll, NGR NR 747766. The directional daylight from the cave mouth clearly showed the carved relief cross on the wall above the 'altar'. TE Gray, neg no 3431/1, May 1987.*

GLOSSARY

APERTURE The hole within the lens which is modified by means of the blades of the iris diaphragm, similar to the iris in the eye, thus giving control of the amount of light which reaches the film. Lens apertures are given an f-number, a large aperture might for our work be f/5.6, suitable for a single stone, a very small aperture being f/22, which might be used for the stone in its landscape setting. See DEPTH OF FIELD.

AUTO COMPACT CAMERAS Such cameras automatically take care of LENS APERTURE and SHUTTER SPEED, ensuring correct exposure, and focussing is also automatic. They are of limited use in sculpture photography because there is seldom a flash socket to allow the fitting of long leads to fire remote flashes, and because the inbuilt flash gives too flat a light to provide relief and contrast to shallow carving. They could be very useful for subjects where one can be there when the sunlight is at the correct angle, and for photographing stones in their landscape settings.

BRACKETING A way of not losing opportunities, used mostly with transparency film which is sensitive to small variations in exposure. After the metered exposure is given, another exposure is made at one stop smaller, and a third at one stop larger, the best transparency being selected later.

CONTRAST The relative difference between the darkest and lightest parts of a subject. A spotlit stage scene with impenetrable shadows and brilliant highlights is of a very high contrast, the brilliantly lit parts getting perhaps 50 times as much light as the shadows. A landscape in cloudy conditions is of low contrast. Film has a limited ability to handle wide contrast ranges. A sunny landscape with white clouds exhibits the range of contrast which photo materials can handle well, and in this situation the light which falls on the sunlit parts is found to have four times the strength of the light reaching the shadows. This is the 4–1 ideal for which we aim when using flash to light the main area of a stone, balancing this by the use of daylight to fill in the shadows.

DEPTH OF FIELD The distance between the nearest and farthest parts of a subject which appear in sharp detail in the photograph. A tiny lens aperture of f/22 gives very great depth of field, a large aperture of f/5.6 gives very little depth of field. With shots of single stones a large depth of field is not usually necessary, but where the stone is set in an attractive landscape a smaller aperture with greater depth of field would be more appropriate to do justice to the scene.

FLARE If bright light from the sun or other light shines in the lens it can create bright patterns on the negative, usually the shape of the hole in the diaphragm within the lens. A more insidious effect is an overall veil of density on the negative which considerably lowers its contrast. As much of the time in our work the flashes are forward of the camera and almost on the same plane as the subject, there is a distinct danger of flare from the light reaching the lens. The most effective way to eradicate this is by means of BARN DOORS on the flashes, much more effective than a lens hood, although that should be used as an additional insurance.

FILM SPEEDS Regrettably, four different systems are currently in use to indicate film speeds: ASA from the American Standards Association, ISO from the Swiss-based International Standards Organisation, Exposure Index (EI) from Kodak, and the German system DIN. The first three systems are arithmetical, ie 400 film speed is twice as fast as 200 film speed. DIN is a logarithmic system, ie a speed of 24 DIN is twice as fast as 21 DIN. Virtually all films are now marked in DIN speeds, in addition to ASA, ISO or EI.

The majority of cameras and exposure meters are at present scaled in ASA and some with DIN as well; only the most recently produced equipment is scaled in ISO speeds. It is likely to be some time, perhaps years, before the photographic industry is fully standardized in one system, which may well be ISO.

All this apparent confusion will become clear, because any film will have the same film speed in all three arithmetical systems (ASA, ISO, EI). Thus a film speed of EI 400 or ISO 400 can be transferred with perfect confidence to a camera or meter dial calibrated in ASA. If film and camera or meter are marked in DIN, there is no problem in using that system.

LENS HOOD These can be purchased to fit a wide range of cameras and lenses and are intended to prevent bright light reaching the lens thus creating FLARE.

SHUTTER SPEED Camera shutters are calibrated in fractions of a second, ie 1/30th, 1/60th, etc.

Shutter speeds and lens APERTURES are marked in such a way that each setting represents a halving or doubling of the light that reaches the film. For example, 1/250th at f/8, 1/125th at f/11, and 1/60th at f/16 all result in the same quantity of light reaching the film, the only difference being that f/16 would give much greater DEPTH OF FIELD than f/8.

ACKNOWLEDGEMENTS

I have been aided in my work by many museum curators and estate owners, in particular Mike Spearman of the National Museums of Scotland, Mike King of Fife Museums, Norman Atkinson of Angus Museums, Jocelyn Chamberlain-Mole of Peterhead Museum, Christine Sangster formerly of Elgin Museum, Robin Hanley of Inverness Museum, Elizabeth Marshall formerly of Groam House Museum, Lord Strathnaver at Dunrobin, and the Thurso Museum Trust. Graham Ritchie, Lesley Ferguson and Iain Fraser of RCAHMS were and are enormously supportive. Regional archaeologists were always helpful, and in addition many useful suggestions came from Charles Thomas, Leslie Alcock, Isabel Henderson and Edwina Proudfoot. The lighting techniques that I use are a modification of that developed many years ago for photographing the recumbent stones of Argyll, by Geoff Quick, formerly Principal Photographer of RCAHMS.

I would see little point in encouraging people to record stones if these records were not to be readily accessible to scholars, and I am grateful to Lesley Ferguson for her contribution on creating an archive. My thanks also to Ian Gray, formerly of Historic Scotland, who supplied the drawings.

I am grateful to my fellow members of the National Committee on the Carved Stones of Scotland for their support and many helpful suggestions which made my text much more readable, especially Anna Ritchie for her expert and sensitive editing, but any remaining mistakes are mine.

RECORDING CARVED STONES AND THE NATIONAL MONUMENTS RECORD OF SCOTLAND

LESLEY M FERGUSON, RCAHMS

'We were fortunate, after long exposure by magnesium wire or ribbon, in procuring a remarkable photograph of this spirited symbol; and, at another time, my father made a stucco cast of it, which, for many years, adorned the drawingroom grate of my early home during the fireless days of summer.'

So wrote Jessie Patrick Findlay in an illustrated essay written to compete for the Society of Antiquaries of Scotland Chalmers-Jervise prize, in which she describes assisting her father John Patrick in 1902 to photograph the symbols carved in the caves at East Wemyss, Fife. The carvings had first been discovered in 1865 by Sir James Young Simpson, who had described them in the *Proceedings of the Royal Society of Edinburgh*, and they were later illustrated by others, but John Patrick was the first person to use the relatively new medium of photography to record the symbols. Publishing some of his photographs in *The Reliquary and Illustrated Archaeologist*, Patrick's enthusiasm and fascination for the symbols is apparent throughout the text, feelings shared by his daughter and numerous other

19 *East Wemyss, Dovecot Cave, Fife, NGR NT 343970. Stucco cast of Pictish symbol made by John Patrick, 1902. NMRS, neg no B35180.*

people who have in the past spent many happy hours recording in various forms all the different types of carved stones (illus 19).

The photographs of John Patrick and the typescript of Jessie Patrick Findlay are held in the collections of the National Monuments Record of Scotland (NMRS), an integral part of the Royal Commission on the Ancient and Historical Monuments of Scotland (RCAHMS), who have been responsible since 1908 for creating an inventory of archaeological sites, monuments and buildings. Currently, the NMRS holds information on more than 100,000 archaeological sites, monuments and buildings in Scotland, as well as curating a vast collection of photographs, drawings, manuscripts, books and aerial photographs relating to the past. Material in the collections ranges in date from the late 17th century through to the 1990s, and it is constantly being enlarged as new accessions are received. New sites (including carved stones) are also recorded on a daily basis from a variety of sources. These include sites discovered during the course of RCAHMS fieldwork or aerial photography, sites reported in publications such as *Discovery and Excavation in Scotland* (*DES*), and sites described in letters from local researchers.

Photography was used in the early years of RCAHMS fieldwork, although it was not until 1957 that the first professional photographer was appointed and a photographic department established. The techniques used in photographing carved stones had changed considerably since the methods described by John Patrick, but there were still difficulties, particularly in dealing with eroded stones in poor daylight. RCAHMS photographers tried various methods in the 1960s and 1970s to get better results, including wetting carved stones to create more contrast, circling stones with a hand lamp during a long exposure to highlight the raised details, and taking photographs at night using artificial light at oblique angles (Quick 1975). Through this process of experimentation, a system was developed and perfected using synchronized flash photography at oblique angles. Many of the resulting photographs were published in *Late Medieval Monumental Sculpture in the West Highlands* by KA Steer and J Bannerman, and in the Argyll Inventories. The photographic equipment has changed and developed, but this is still the system in use today by RCAHMS for recording carved stones, and it forms the basis of the methods described by Tom E Gray in this booklet.

Studying and recording any form of carved stone is still a very worthwhile and rewarding occupation, whether prehistoric cup-and-ring markings, Pictish symbol stones, early Christian stones, medieval graveslabs, architectural fragments or 18th-century gravestones. It is also very important, for it provides a record of a particular stone or stones within an area, at a certain point in time. Despite the wealth of knowledge built up over the years, there are still carved stones which have not been fully recorded, and there are many awaiting discovery. In *DES 1995* alone, there were over 60 new stones (including cup-markings) reported, and, although 11 of these were fragments from one excavation at Kirriemuir, the figure is indicative of the potential. Through the years there are stones which have been 'lost', often moved, forgotten, or which have become

20 *Inverallan, Moray, NGR NJ 026260. This symbol stone was photographed by James Ritchie in 1910 (left), and again in 1990 by Tom E Gray (right). In the eighty-year gap between the taking of these photographs, there has been considerable erosion of the stone face, and the stone has been moved to a different location. These two prints clearly illustrate the importance of having photographs taken at different points in time. NMRS neg no A8685; TE Gray neg no 3688/2.*

overgrown, and again various entries in *DES 1995* state 'originally found in 1870... lost for several years... it was rediscovered in 1988' or 'the fragment... noticed in the Manse rockery in 1984, and since lost, was rediscovered.' A carved stone should not be precluded from further recording, just because it has already been photographed or drawn.

It is important that we build up a record of carved stones, which will help to illustrate the history of each stone, including any movement or damage, or even just to assist in the individual identification where several similar stones are known. Historic Scotland has outlined some of the problems facing carved stones in a leaflet, *The Carved Stones of Scotland. A Guide to Helping in their Protection.* These problems include damage through exposure to the elements, very clearly demonstrated by the stone at Inverallan, Moray. This Pictish stone was photographed in 1910 by James Ritchie, and in 1990, using the techniques described in this publication, by Tom Gray. Comparison of the two photographs clearly indicates considerable erosion of the stone since 1910, as well as a change in position, the earlier photograph showing the stone next to a wall, at a slight angle, whereas by 1990 the stone had been moved and was built into the graveyard wall (illus 20).

21 *Clatt, Aberdeenshire, NGR NJ 538260. The larger of the two symbol stones is built into a wall, but the fragment to the left of the 'beast' photographed by James Ritchie in 1905 has since disappeared. NMRS neg no A8675.*

Examination of references in 19th-century books and looking through the collections in the NMRS provide tantalising glimpses of numerous examples of stones which have disappeared or been moved since they were first recorded. Photographed in 1905 by James Ritchie, the Pictish stone with a 'beast' which is built on its side into a wall at Clatt, Aberdeenshire, has a fragment of another stone lying loose beside it, the whereabouts of which is not now known (illus 21). Other examples include the Lindores Stone, which was illustrated by James Skene in his manuscript album of 1832 titled *Drawings of the ancient sculptured monuments still existing in Scotland, as they presently appear* (illus 22). The stone is described in notes as 'now lying prostrate on the summit of a wooded knoll near the road side close to the village.' It is known that this stone came from the crest of a nearby hill and was later built into a garden wall at Lindores, before being moved to the Old Mort House at Abdie Churchyard. Fortunately in this instance, the movement of the stone is documented.

In recent years, professional excavation has preceded any movement of stones scheduled by Historic Scotland, and a written and photographic record has been made of each stone, in order that successive generations will be able to understand its history. At Fowlis Wester, prior to the removal of a cross-slab into the parish church, excavation demonstrated that the stone had been moved on a previous occasion, but there is no record to indicate when this happened.

The excitement of the discovery of carvings has in some instances been well documented. To return to Jessie Patrick Findlay in the East Wemyss caves:

'On the eastern, dimly-lighted wall of that cave there awaited us the crown of our quest for symbols - the discovery of a large and clear carving of a hitherto unrecorded form. Although I was the first to see it, it was not with the discerning eye of the archaeologist. That honour was reserved for my father who was photographing some markings on another wall while I wandered round and stumbled on "the great discovery". In my haste to inform him of it, I waved my candle too enthusiastically so that the flame was extinguished, leaving me groping, with all

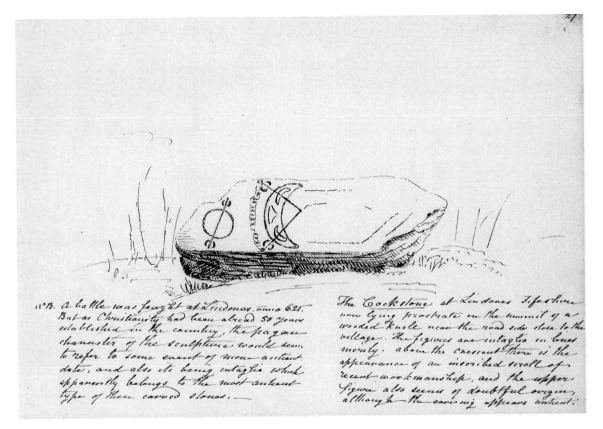

27

No 13. A battle was fought at Lindores anno 621. But as Christianity had been abroad 50 years established in the country, the pagan character of the sculptures would seem to refer to some event of more ancient date, and also its being intaglio which apparently belongs to the most ancient type of these carved stones. —

The Cockstone at Lindores Fifeshire now lying prostrate on the summit of a wooded knoll near the road side close to the village. The figures are intaglio in lines merely. above the crescent there is the appearance of an inscribed scroll of recent workmanship, and the upper figure also seems of doubtful origin, although the carving appears ancient.

22 Lindores, Fife, NGR NO 261169. Drawn by James Skene in 1832, the position of the stone at that date is described. NMRS neg no FID/389/1.

sense of direction hopelessly lost.... Hastily relighting my candle I announced my "find" in flippant tones. "I have discovered a new symbol! – It's neither a Sun-Mansion nor a Sun-Snake. It looks like a Sun-centipede! – Or the skeleton of the whale that swallowed Jon–." "It's a Viking Ship!" cried my father who had sufficient faith to hurry to the spot. "What a find! ...". (Illus 23)

Other discoveries have been illustrated visually, as here at Tillytarmont, Aberdeenshire, where a Pictish stone with an eagle and beast carving was uncovered by the farmer while ploughing in 1972 (illus 24). It is one of several Pictish stones recovered from the field since the 1860s.

All these examples represent a very small part of the NMRS collections, but should give an indication of the importance and value of having a record of carved stones. In the NMRS, we would welcome the deposition of any photographs or other material, such as notes, sketches, drawings

23 East Wemyss, Jonathan's Cave, Fife, NGR NT 345972. The boat carved on the cave wall as photographed at the time of its discovery by John Patrick, 1902. NMRS neg no F/8286.

24 *Tillytarmont, Banffshire, NGR NJ 533472. This Pictish symbol stone was uncovered during ploughing in 1972. NMRS neg no B75938.*

and so on, that would complement our existing collection and build up the visual record of carved stones. The material need not necessarily be modern, but could be examples from earlier years, for example, photographs from a family album from the 1900s.

Coupled with the role of collecting material and making information available, the NMRS has the responsibility to ensure that the collections will still be available for future research, and therefore conservation is of prime importance. The collections are stored in archivally stable conditions appropriate to the nature of different types of material.

Before the start of any survey, it is worthwhile carrying out some research to find out what is already known about a stone (if anything), and whether it is listed or scheduled. It is also essential to speak to the landowner to obtain permission to take photographs. The recording of stones

must not involve any action which might have a detrimental effect, such as digging into the ground, lifting or moving stones, or taking rubbings.

Taking the photographs is only part of the recording process. Other details are necessary to provide an essential and accurate record, which will be of considerable value both now and in the future. Betty Willsher describes in detail the best approach for surveying graveyards in *How to Record Scottish Graveyards*, and she recommends the use of a monument form with various categories for accurate recording. The booklet is full of useful information on surveying techniques, which apply more widely than graveyards, and it is an invaluable guide for anyone considering recording carved stones.

There are some basic details which may seem obvious but which are a vital part of any recording process, particularly for more isolated stones. A recording form has been designed to assist with these details; you will find it at the end of this booklet, and it can be photocopied for use while you are examining the stone. A form has been completed, as an example, for the stone at Farnell in Angus. The following notes are for guidance.

a. First of all, the most important information to note is the location of the stone or stones. A place-name is necessary but is not on its own sufficient, and the National Grid Reference (NGR) is vital to record the position accurately. If a large-scale (1:1250, 1:2500, 1:10,000) Ordnance Survey map is available, it can be annotated with a cross to mark the location. Taped measurements to permanent features marked on the map, such as corners of buildings, junctions of walls etc, can provide a mechanism with which to double-check the details and which will allow someone unfamiliar with the area to find the stone/s. Sketch plans are also of considerable use.

b. A general description of the object, including details of what type of carved stone is being recorded, whether cup-and-ring marking, Pictish symbol stone, cross-incised stone, architectural fragment, gravestone etc; whether it is a free-standing stone, or a carving on a natural rock outcrop; whether the carving is incised or in relief; whether there is an inscription and if so what it reads; wherever possible, the metric measurements (height, width and depth) of the stone, accompanied by a sketch.

c. The archaeological history of the stone is important. If it was discovered recently, we need to know how it was found and who found it.

d. If there is an immediate threat to the stone, for example from the demolition of a wall, contact should be made as soon as possible with the Council Archaeologist or Historic Scotland.

e. Recording undertaken. Reference numbers identifying the photographs taken are essential, along with descriptive details, for example 'stone viewed from west' or 'detailed view of mirror symbol'. The reference number can either be in the form of a film and frame number, or, if large numbers of photographs are being taken, a separate numbering system. It is best to avoid annotating the backs of photographic prints with too much detail; the film/frame numbers should suffice and this must be done in a soft pencil, as ink can 'bleed' through the photograph and destroy the image.

The NMRS is always interested to hear about new discoveries or to have further information on known sites which can be added to the database, and to receive copies of photographs or other material to add to the Collections. Staff are pleased to advise and to discuss any records you may have made, and we can be contacted at John Sinclair House, 16 Bernard Terrace, Edinburgh, EH8 9NX, telephone 0131 662 1456, fax 0131 662 1477/1499. The NMRS is open for public consultation from Monday to Friday (9.30–4.30, 4.00 on Fridays), and anyone interested in examining the collections or finding out more about any aspect of Scotland's archaeology or architecture is very welcome.

References and Further Reading

There seems to be little on the specialist subject of photographing sculpture, except for the valuable contributions from Quick and Willsher.

Allen, J Romilly, and Anderson, J 1903
The Early Christian Monuments of Scotland, Edinburgh.
A facsimile edition in 1993 by Pinkfoot Press, Balgavies, by Forfar, Angus, DD8 2TH. The 'bible' for anyone interested in Dark Age sculpture.

British Photographers' Liaison Committeee
Photographers' Guide to the 1988 Copyright Act. The British Photographers' Liaison Committee, 9–10 Domingo Street, London, EC1 OTA.
Amendments on copyright for photographers are still under discussion, which leaves the above a little out of date, but it is a useful guide and will no doubt be updated.

Buchanan, Terry 1983
Photographing Historic Buildings, HMSO London.
Deals with sculptural fragments as well as the broader field of architecture.

Council for British Archaeology 1987
Recording Worked Stones, Practical Handbook No 1, London.
Has a useful little piece on photography.

Findlay, J 1905
'The sculptured caves of East Wemyss', *The Reliquary and Illustrated Archaeologist*, n.s., Vol 11: part 1, 73–84; part 2, 49–63.

Findlay, J 1906
'The sculptured caves of East Wemyss', *The Reliquary and Illustrated Archaeologist*, n.s., Vol 12: part 3, 37–47.

Findlay, J P 1924
'Some vestiges of forgotten Fife – The caves of Wemyss'. Unpublished essay written to compete for the Chalmers Jervise Prize, Society of Antiquaries of Scotland.

Gray, T E 1988
'Correcting verticals under the enlarger', *The Photographic Journal*, December 1988.

Historic Scotland
The Carved Stones of Scotland. A Guide to Helping in their Protection.
Leaflet available free from Historic Scotland.

Quick, G B 1975
'The photography of relief carving', *The Photographic Journal*, June 1975, 272–7.
Deals specifically with lighting the recumbent monuments of Argyll to reveal worn detail. Applicable, modified, to much other sculpture.

Simpson, J Y 1866
'Notice of some ancient sculptures on the walls of caves in Fife', *Proceedings of the Royal Society of Edinburgh*, 2 (1862–6), 521–6.

Skene, J 1832
Drawings of the ancient sculptured monuments still existing in Scotland, as they presently appear. Unpublished manuscript, Society of Antiquaries of Scotland Collection, NMRS.

Willsher, Betty 1985
How to record Scottish Graveyards, Council for Scottish Archaeology, Edinburgh.
Includes a thoroughly practical guide to photographing later medieval and post-Reformation gravestones.

Historic Scotland
Longmore House
Salisbury Place
Edinburgh EH9 1SH

telephone 0131 662 1250

National Committee on the Carved
Stones of Scotland
c/o Society of Antiquaries of Scotland
Royal Museum of Scotland
Chambers Street
Edinburgh EH1 1JF

telephone 0131 225 7534

Royal Commission on the Ancient and
Historical Monuments of Scotland
National Monuments Record of Scotland
John Sinclair House
16 Bernard Terrace
Edinburgh EH8 9NX

telephone 0131 662 1456

NATIONAL COMMITTEE ON THE CARVED STONES OF SCOTLAND

Scotland has a great wealth of carved stones from prehistoric cup-and-ring-marked stones, Roman sculpture, the symbol stones and cross-slabs of the Picts, the early medieval monuments of the Scots, Northumbrians and Britons, Romanesque and Gothic sculpture, from medieval churches, and late medieval grave-slabs, to more recent grave-stones and architectural sculpture. Many are of immense importance for archaeology, national and local history, the history of society, and as works of art.

These stones face many threats: Scotland's climate; acid rain and other pollution; surface growth; traffic; cattle; destruction and redevelopment of sites and buildings; vandalism; theft; stone-rubbing; or well-intentioned but potentially destructive cleaning, repair and restoration.

Historic Scotland has launched an important programme of research into the decay of carved stones. In the context of this research and of growing public interest in Scotland's carved stones, Historic Scotland has set up a National Committee on Carved Stones in Scotland to consider how they should best be protected.

The Committee aims to increase awareness of the importance of Scotland's carved stones and of the threats that face them. It is hoped that it will act as a forum for co-ordinating programmes for recording and protecting these stones.

Royal Commission on the Ancient and Historical Monuments of Scotland
John Sinclair House
16 Bernard Terrace
Edinburgh EH8 9NX

Tel. 0131 - 662 1456   Fax. 0131 - 662 1477

CARVED STONE RECORDING FORM

Stone location

Place name   FARNELL PARISH CHURCH   Parish   FARNELL

NGR   NO 627 554   Local authority   ANGUS

Sketch

Stone is built into outer face of S wall of church, 0.5m E of second buttress from SE corner, and 0.35m above ground level.

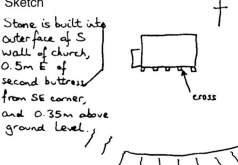

cross

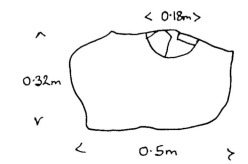

< 0.18m >

0.32m

0.5m

General description

A block of dressed red sandstone, 0.5m long and 0.32m high, bearing what appears to be a portion of a consecration cross. This is incised, and is formed by intersecting arcs, meeting in a central disc, the whole contained within an outer circle.

History of stone

Date recorded 9th March 1996   Who recorded it   I Fraser

How was it found? Examination of walls of church

Threat

Threat of possible damage from debris stacked against wall of church.

Recording

Type of recording undertaken Photography and measured sketch.

Film number 1996/4   Frame number 24, 25   Description

Royal Commission on the Ancient and Historical Monuments of Scotland
John Sinclair House
16 Bernard Terrace
Edinburgh EH8 9NX
Tel. 0131 - 662 1456   Fax. 0131 - 662 1477

CARVED STONE RECORDING FORM

Stone location

Place name

Parish

NGR

Local authority

Sketch

General description

History of stone

Date recorded

Who recorded it

How was it found?

Threat

Recording

Type of recording undertaken

Film number   Frame number   Description

Please continue overleaf

25 *Pictish symbol stone at Broomend of Crichie, Aberdeenshire, NGR NJ 779197. TE Gray. neg no 3575/1.*